faithful
to the end

2 TIMOTHY

by Mark Mulryne

faithful to the end
the good book guide to 2 timothy
© Mark Mulryne/The Good Book Company, 2007. Reprinted 2012.
Series Consultants: Tim Chester, Tim Thornborough,
                              Anne Woodcock, Carl Laferton

The Good Book Company
Tel (UK): 0333-225-0880
Tel (int): + (44) 208-942-0880
Tel: (US): 866 244 2165
Email: admin@thegoodbook.co.uk

Websites
UK: www.thegoodbook.co.uk
N America: www.thegoodbook.com
Australia: www.thegoodbook.com.au
New Zealand: www.thegoodbook.co.nz

ISBN: 9781905564569

Printed in China

CONTENTS

introduction: good book guides

Every Bible-study group is different—yours may take place in a church building, in a home or in a cafe, on a train, over a leisurely mid-morning coffee or squashed into a 30-minute lunch break. Your group may include new Christians, mature Christians, non-Christians, mums and tots, students, businessmen or teens. That's why we've designed these *Good Book Guides* to be flexible for use in many different situations.

Our aim in each session is to uncover the meaning of a passage, and see how it fits into the "big picture" of the Bible. But that can never be the end. We also need to appropriately apply what we have discovered to our lives. Let's take a look at what is included:

⊕ **Talkabout:** Most groups need to "break the ice" at the beginning of a session, and here's the question that will do that. It's designed to get people talking around a subject that will be covered in the course of the Bible study.

⬇ **Investigate:** The Bible text for each session is broken up into manageable chunks, with questions that aim to help you understand what the passage is about. **The Leader's Guide** contains **guidance on questions**, and sometimes ⊠ additional "follow-up" questions.

⊡ **Explore more (optional):** These questions will help you connect what you have learned to other parts of the Bible, so you can begin to fit it all together like a jig-saw; or occasionally look at a part of the passage that's not dealt with in detail in the main study.

⊡ **Apply:** As you go through a Bible study, you'll keep coming across **apply** sections. These are questions to get the group discussing what the Bible teaching means in practice for you and your church. ⊡ **Getting personal** is an opportunity for you to think, plan and pray about the changes that you personally may need to make as a result of what you have learned.

⬆ **Pray:** We want to encourage prayer that is rooted in God's word—in line with His concerns, purposes and promises. So each session ends with an opportunity to review the truths and challenges highlighted by the Bible study, and turn them into prayers of request and thanksgiving.

The **Leader's Guide** and introduction provide historical background information, explanations of the Bible texts for each session, ideas for **optional extra** activities, and guidance on how best to help people uncover the truths of God's word.

why study 2 Timothy?

Last words can be significant—they can reveal what is ultimately most important for the speaker. In Paul's second letter to Timothy, we have the last written words known to us of the apostle Paul. As he wrote, Paul was in prison, facing the end of his life, cut off from the churches that he had set up, and deserted by most of his gospel co-workers, to whom he had become an object of shame. Christians had become intimidated by the apparent success of opposition to the gospel from those outside the church. Meanwhile, inside the church, false teaching was spreading and many people seemed to like what they heard.

It would be easy to panic in a situation like this—or to go into survival mode: keep your head down and do as little as possible to antagonise your opponents or confront the false teachers. But Paul knew that the only way to guard the precious gospel of Jesus Christ was to teach it to the next generation of leaders and teachers, who, in turn, could pass it on to the succeeding generations. So Paul writes this deeply personal letter to Timothy, the man who was to become his spiritual "heir", and would take the gospel to the next generation.

He writes to both challenge and encourage Timothy—to preach the word, to keep his head in all situations, to endure hardship, to fight the good fight and run the race to the very end.

The church today is still only one generation from extinction. The world is opposed to Jesus Christ, and false teachers seem to run rampant, destroying faith and denying God's power. Inside and outside church, people ridicule, intimidate and oppose anyone who sticks to the Bible. And like Timothy, we all feel the pressure to be ashamed of the gospel. We can all be disturbed by the word of God, which rebukes and corrects us—we can all be attracted by false teachings that suit our own powerful desires instead.

These seven studies have been written to help Christians who feel demoralised, cowardly, and tempted to be ashamed of the gospel. As we investigate this letter, we can stand in Timothy's shoes, listening to the encouragements and the commands of the battle-scarred apostle. We will learn the boldness of his plan for the gospel and the boldness of his attitude to opposition, even when he was right in the thick of it. We will be reminded of the utter faithfulness of Jesus Christ, the wonder of the gospel, the certainty of Christ's return and judgment, the power of Scripture to save us and equip us for every good work, and the joy of what we look forward to—the unique Christian hope.

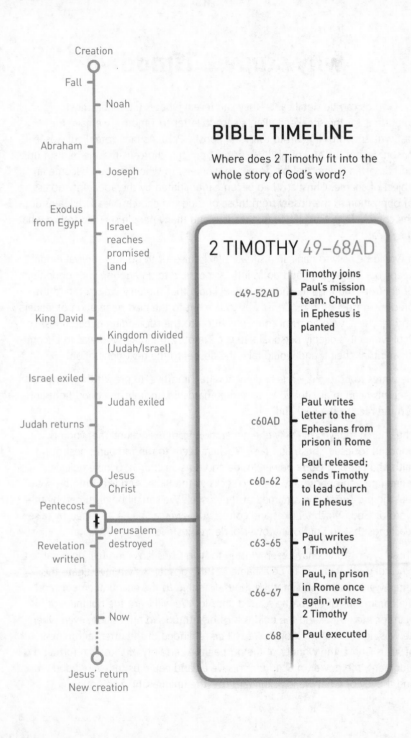

Creation
Fall
Noah
Abraham
Joseph
Exodus from Egypt
Israel reaches promised land

BIBLE TIMELINE

Where does 2 Timothy fit into the whole story of God's word?

2 TIMOTHY 49–68AD

King David
Kingdom divided (Judah/Israel)
Israel exiled
Judah exiled
Judah returns
Jesus Christ
Pentecost
Jerusalem destroyed
Revelation written
Now
Jesus' return
New creation

c49-52AD	Timothy joins Paul's mission team. Church in Ephesus is planted
c60AD	Paul writes letter to the Ephesians from prison in Rome
c60-62	Paul released; sends Timothy to lead church in Ephesus
c63-65	Paul writes 1 Timothy
c66-67	Paul, in prison in Rome once again, writes 2 Timothy
c68	Paul executed

1 Overview
WHAT'S 2 TIMOTHY ALL ABOUT?

⊕ talkabout

1. If you could plan your last words, what would you like to say?

⊕ investigate

Timothy was a younger Christian leader who had accompanied Paul on some of his missionary journeys. Paul later sent him to help lead churches Paul had started. When Paul writes this letter, Timothy is probably still leading and teaching the church in Ephesus. Paul, however, knows he himself is coming to the end of his life—he expects to be executed as part of the persecution of Christians going on at the time. So what are Paul's final instructions to Timothy? What is his final message to the believers who have heard the gospel though his preaching? Read on to find out!

2. **Read 2 Timothy 1 v 2-5.** What does Paul think of Timothy now?

3. **Read 1 v 15-17, 2 v 9 and 4 v 16.** What is Paul's situation?

4. **Read 2 v 17-18.** What is the situation in the church?

5. **Read 3 v 13 and 4 v 3-4.** What things are expected in the future?

⊖ **apply**

6. If you were Paul, what sort of things might be going through your mind as you faced this situation?

- How similar are the problems facing the church today (both locally and worldwide)?

- What sort of things do you hope to learn from Paul as you study this letter?

⊌ investigate

7. **Read 1 v 13-14.** What is Paul's big concern?

8. **Read 2 v 2.** What is Paul's plan for achieving this?

⊡ explore more

optional

What actually is the message of the gospel?

▸ **Read John 3 v 16**

Try to construct an outline of the good news. What do these verses tell us about...
- *God?*
- *ourselves?*
- *Jesus and His death?*
- *faith?*
- *the alternative?*

Now see if you can explain what the gospel is in your own words.

9. **Read 2 v 25-26.** What else will Paul's plan involve for Timothy?

10. **Read 1 v 8 and 3 v 12.** What will happen to Timothy in the process?

• What is Paul worried that Timothy might do (1 v 8)?

⮕ apply

11. If you were Timothy, what sort of things might be going through your mind?

• How similar are the experiences of Christians today (both locally and worldwide)?

• What sort of things do you hope to learn along with Timothy as you study this letter?

⊕ investigate

12. **Read 1 v 9-10.** What's the biggest encouragement to Timothy to still do his job?

⊡ getting personal

When you became a Christian, or as you grew up in a Christian family, what did you think the Christian life would be like? Did you realise that living for Jesus will mean suffering? Are you prepared for any challenges that may lie ahead?

⊕ pray

As a group:

Thank God for faithful and fearless teachers of His word through the ages, such as Paul. Pray for the leaders of your church and their God-given responsibilities.

On your own:

Think again about what you hope to gain from this Bible-study course. Ask God to help you grow in faithfulness and fearlessness as you live for Christ in this hostile world.

> **BEFORE NEXT TIME**

- **READ AHEAD:** 2 Timothy 1 v 1-10

- **THINK AHEAD:** *What things will keep Timothy going in his difficult job?*

2 2 Timothy 1 v 1-10
FANNING THE FLAME

The story so far

As the next generation of the church, our most important task is to guard the gospel from change, and pass it on to the following generation.

⊕ talkabout

1. Imagine you have a friend who is a Christian leader, and whose job is turning out to be a bit of a nightmare because of opposition from inside and outside the church. How might you try to encourage them?

⊕ investigate

Paul is in prison in Rome, and is probably going to be executed. Timothy has assisted Paul in preaching the gospel message for years, but is now in leadership at the church in Ephesus. Paul is writing to Timothy with what might be final instructions of what to do when he's gone. So how is he going to start his final message?

▶ Read 2 Timothy 1 v 1-10

2. When Paul sets aside time to pray for Timothy, what things come into his head (v 3-5)?

DICTIONARY

Apostle (v 1): someone chosen and sent by Jesus to serve the church.
Grace (v 2,9): undeserved kindness.
Laying on of hands (v 6): the way the early church publicly appointed people to a particular role in the church.
Holy (v 9): set apart; totally pure.
Immortality (v 10): eternity with God.

3. Paul is about to give Timothy a challenge (v 6-8). What does Paul do first to encourage him?

• verses 3-4:

• verse 5:

4. In verse 6, Paul challenges Timothy to keep using the gift of teaching and leadership that God has given him. What does this picture of fanning a flame tell us about Timothy's gift and what he needed to do?

5. What powerful reason does Paul give Timothy to work at using his God-given gift (v 7)?

6. Why might Timothy be "ashamed" of the gospel?

• Why is being ashamed of Paul so close to being ashamed of the gospel, do you think?

7. What sort of power does God offer to overcome this shame, according to verse 8?

⤷ apply

8. What things can tempt us to be ashamed of the gospel (or of true gospel teachers)?

9. How does Paul's understanding of "the power of God" (v 8b) differ from that of many people today?

⊡ explore more

optional

2 Timothy 1 v 8 mentions "suffering for the gospel, by the power of God". This link between suffering and God's power would surprise most people today—it's not what usually comes to mind when we think of God's power. But the New Testament gives a very different picture.

▶ Read John 12 v 23-33

What event is Jesus talking about here?

What does Jesus say to show that this event would mean shame and suffering for Him?

How would it show the power of God?

What does Jesus say about His followers here?

How much do you really want the sort of power of God that Paul speaks about in verse 8—the power to suffer for the gospel? It's a hard thing to pray for! But it's something we need if we are going to do God's work.

⊡ **investigate**

10. Re-read verses 9-10. Why are the Lord and His gospel worth suffering for?

⊡ **apply**

11. Can you explain what God has done for you in Jesus Christ? Why not have a go, using verses 9-10?

12. How can we avoid being ashamed, and instead, carry out God's command to pass on His message to others?

13. How can we encourage our church leaders not to give up on this task? Look again at your answers to Question One. Would you make any changes to the way in which you go about encouraging "your friend"?

⊕ **pray**

Pray for the "spirit of power [to suffer], of love and of self-control". Pray this for your Christian leaders, for yourselves, and for the persecuted church worldwide.

▶ **BEFORE NEXT TIME**

- **READ AHEAD:** 2 Timothy 1 v 11-18
- **THINK AHEAD:** *How will Timothy be encouraged by Paul's own example and that of Onesiphorus?*

3 2 Timothy 1 v 11-18
GUARDING THE GOSPEL

The story so far

As the next generation of the church, our most important task is to guard the gospel from change, and pass it on to the following generation.

Christians shouldn't be ashamed of the gospel! We can and must stand up for it, even when that means suffering.

⊕ talkabout

1. What do you think is the most important job of the church? Share some of the different ideas that you have come across, both inside and outside the church.

⊕ investigate

Paul has been telling Timothy to stand up for the gospel message about Jesus—he should not be ashamed of it, but use his gift to preach it, and, if necessary, suffer for it. Paul encourages him to do this by reminding him of how God has worked in his life in the past, of the power that God can give him, and of how amazing the gospel message is. And there is more encouragement to come...

> **Read 2 Timothy 1 v 11-18**

DICTIONARY

Herald (v 11): announcer.
Entrusted (v 12, 14): given to, trusted with.

2. What was Paul's own experience of being a gospel teacher?

3. How can he be so positive about his experience, despite the circumstances?

4. Why does Paul describe his difficult experiences as a gospel teacher, do you think?

optional

⊡ explore more

Paul suffered enormously for preaching about Jesus.

> **Read 2 Corinthians 11 v 24-33**

How might Paul have been tempted to respond to these painful experiences?

See also **2 Corinthians 4 v 17-18**, where Paul describes his weak body as a "jar of clay" and Jesus Christ, who is at work in his weak body, as "treasure".

What kept Paul going through weakness and suffering?

How might this encourage us, when we feel weak during times of hardship?

In the middle of this section, Paul gives Timothy a big command (v 13-14). Although there are two instructions, they are talking about the same thing. "The pattern of sound teaching" (v 13) and "the good deposit that was entrusted to you" (v 14) both refer to the gospel message about Jesus Christ, and the implications it has for our lives. Each command helps to explain what the other means. The reason for keeping "the pattern of sound teaching" is to guard "the good deposit" (the gospel message): the way to guard the gospel is to keep "the pattern of sound teaching".

5. Look at verse 13. What does Timothy need to do if he is to keep the pattern of sound teaching?

6. Look at verse 14. What does Timothy need if he is to "guard the good deposit"?

• Why is that essential, do you think?

7. Put Paul's big command in verses 13-14 into your own words.

→ apply

8. Which parts of the gospel do we especially need to guard, because they are under threat today?

9. Why do you think that many churches have given up teaching the gospel like this?

• What could you say to those who believe that Paul's big command is no longer relevant or practical in our modern culture?

10. How can we make sure that the pattern of Paul's teaching is kept by young Christians in our own church and by ourselves?

⊡ **getting personal**

How well do you know the gospel message passed down to us in the Bible from teachers like Paul? Do you know it well enough to recognise threats from false teaching?

⊡ **investigate**

11. How did Onesiphorus show that he was not ashamed of Paul (v 16-17)?

• Why would Onesiphorus' example be a big challenge to Timothy?

→ **apply**

12. How can we follow the example of Onesiphorus today?

⤒ **pray**

For your church and your leaders: that they would guard the gospel message and always keep to the Bible's teaching.

For yourselves: that you would be like Onesiphorus, not ashamed of your gospel teachers, but encouraging them, even through suffering and opposition, to guard the gospel.

▶ **BEFORE NEXT TIME**

• **READ AHEAD:** 2 Timothy 2 v 1-13

• **THINK AHEAD:** *What will Timothy have to do in order to "guard" the gospel?*

4 2 Timothy 2 v 1-13
ENDURING HARDSHIP

The story so far

As the next generation of the church, our most important task is to guard the gospel from change, and pass it on to the following generation.

Christians shouldn't be ashamed of the gospel! We can and must stand up for it, even when that means suffering.

We must guard the gospel by teaching it, as Paul did, and by supporting gospel teachers, as Onesiphorus did, regardless of suffering and shame.

⊕ talkabout

1. Share any experiences you may have had of being a soldier, an athlete, or a farmer. Or talk about what you have learned from the experiences of others—from family or friends, from films or from TV or radio programmes. What do these three roles have in common?

   • What keeps people going in each of these demanding professions?

   We will discover that these jobs will help us understand what it means to "guard the gospel".

⊍ investigate

Paul has been urging Timothy not to be ashamed of telling others about Jesus, and not to be ashamed of Paul, who had been put in prison for doing just that.

❯ Read 2 Timothy 2 v 1-13

2. What is Paul's next instruction to Timothy in verse 1?

• Where is Timothy to find this?

• Why might this be just what Timothy needs to hear?

3. In verse 2, Paul tells Timothy his plan for passing on the gospel message. What are the different links in the chain?

4. Why is this a bold plan in the circumstances?

⊡ apply

5. What should we be doing as a church to make sure there is a next generation of faithful teachers who are able to pass God's message on? Give some practical examples.

⊡ investigate

Paul also wants Timothy to have a bold attitude—and he describes three characters to encourage Timothy to be like this.

6. What can Timothy learn from...
• a soldier (v 3-4)?

• an athlete (v 5)?

• a hardworking farmer (v 6)?

7. What three encouragements in verses 8, 9 and 10 does Paul give Timothy to persevere despite the difficult circumstances?

Verses 11-13 are a reminder that Jesus is always faithful to the promises He has made (see v 13). Paul is especially thinking of the promise to bring all those who keep trusting Jesus Christ safely to heaven.

8. What fear is addressed by the encouragement in verse 11?

9. What fear is addressed by the encouragement in verse 12a?

10. What warning is given in verse 12b?

11. Is verse 13 a warning or an encouragement? How?

• What is the difference between being "faithless" and having "little" or "weak" faith?

explore more

Verses 11 and 12 are a summary of the Christian hope. Read the following New Testament passages. What else are we told about the future that awaits those who have put their trust in Christ?

▶ **Read John 11 v 25-26; 1 Corinthians 15 v 20-28; Revelation 22 v 3-5**

How do these passages make you feel?

⊡ apply

12. When we meet together with our church, what could we do to help other Christians receive the same encouragements and warnings that Paul gives to Timothy? How could we remind each other of...
    • who Jesus is?

    • the power of God's word?

    • the guaranteed success of the gospel?

    • the future of eternal glory?

• the terrible consequences of giving up on Jesus and the gospel?

⊡ getting personal

Which of these encouragements will most help you to be bold in telling others about Jesus?

⊡ pray

Thank God that Jesus Christ will remain faithful, and all that will mean for Christians.

Confess times when you have been weak, you have not remembered Jesus Christ, you have lost sight of eternal glory, or you have given in to temptation to be lazy or comfortable.

Pray that you can "be strong in the grace that is in Christ Jesus"—that you would never disown Jesus, no matter what pressures you face, but that you would always endure in your faith, still trusting in Jesus when you die.

▶ BEFORE NEXT TIME

• **READ AHEAD:** 2 Timothy 2 v 14-26

• **THINK AHEAD:** *How should Timothy react to people who don't faithfully teach God's message?*

5 2 Timothy 2 v 14-26
CORRECTLY HANDLING THE WORD OF TRUTH

The story so far

Christians shouldn't be ashamed of the gospel! We can and must stand up for it, even when that means suffering.

We must guard the gospel by teaching it, as Paul did, and by supporting gospel teachers, as Onesiphorus did, regardless of suffering and shame.

To guard the gospel we must be strong—not in our own strength, but in the grace that is in Jesus Christ.

⊕ talkabout

1. How do you feel and how do you react when people say things that you disagree with?

⬇ investigate

In the first half of chapter 2, Paul challenged Timothy to be strong and to carry out Paul's bold plan to pass the gospel message on, even if it involves suffering. Such strength is possible because of God's power and Jesus' faithfulness to His promises. Now Paul is going to give Timothy more detailed advice about what this will mean in his situation.

> **Read 2 Timothy 2 v 14-26**

> ### DICTIONARY
>
> **Gangrene (v 17):** when an infection causes rapidly spreading death of body tissue.
> **Resurrection (v 18):** here, this refers to the final resurrection, when Jesus returns and all His people are raised for life in His new creation.

2. Try to build up a picture of the problems that were facing the church where Timothy was a leader.
  • verses 16-18

  • verse 14 and verse 23

  • verse 25

The teaching of Hymenaeus and Philetus (v 17-18) seems to have been claiming that the resurrection had "already happened", which would mean that Christians now had everything that they were going to get. This obviously destroys Christian hope.

3. Find words or phrases that Paul uses to describe this false teaching (see v 17 and 26). Why does he take these distortions so seriously?

4. Pick out the three things this false teaching will do in verses 16, 17 and 18.

⤳ apply

5. If people start to believe that there is no future bodily resurrection, because resurrection of some sort has already taken place...
- why will that lead to ungodly behaviour?

- why will others find that an attractive teaching?

- why will that destroy the faith of some people?

6. What other kinds of false teaching might we be in danger from today?

⊡ explore more

optional

❯ Read Matthew 7 v 15-23

Jesus warns His followers about the danger of false prophets (teachers).

What does the picture of wolves in sheep's clothing (v 15) tell us about these people?
How can we recognise false teachers? How long will it take us to recognise them? What are the implications of this?
What kind of things can mislead us into thinking that someone is a godly Christian?
What is the one thing that shows us whether someone is a true follower of Christ?

⊕ investigate

7. ` By contrast with these false teachers, what should be Timothy's aim as a Christian teacher (v 15)?

8. Look at v 14-16 and 23-26. Pick out the specific instructions that Paul gives to Timothy on how to handle false teaching.

• What should Timothy's aim be in his dealings with those spreading false teaching?

⊖ apply

9. How can we help our gospel teachers to deal with false teaching and people who are influenced by it?

⊕ investigate

Paul knows that the presence of false teachers in the church can tempt people into various kinds of wickedness.

10. Why might Timothy (and we) need to hear Paul's warning...
• to cleanse himself from ignoble purposes (v 21)?

• to flee the evil desires of youth (v 22)?

11. From verses 23-26, try to sum up what Timothy's overall strategy should be towards both false teachers and to those prepared to argue over much less serious issues.

• Why was it important for Timothy both to stand up against false views and yet to do this gently?

→ apply

12. If we come across false teaching in our church, what should we do? And what should we avoid doing?

☺ getting personal

Which is the bigger temptation for you—to leave false teaching unchallenged OR to oppose it without kindness and love?

⊤ pray

Look again at your answers in this session and think about how to pray for...

- your church leaders
- false teachers
- those who are deceived by false teaching, who argue about unimportant matters or who oppose your leaders
- yourself

▶ BEFORE NEXT TIME

- **READ AHEAD:** 2 Timothy 3

- **THINK AHEAD:** *What should Timothy expect to face?*
  What should his reaction be?

6 2 Timothy 3
CHOOSING A GODLY LIFE

The story so far

We must guard the gospel by teaching it, as Paul did, and by supporting gospel teachers, as Onesiphorus did, regardless of suffering and shame.

To guard the gospel we must be strong—not in our own strength, but in the grace that is in Jesus Christ.

Guarding the gospel means speaking out against false teaching. But this must be done gently, aiming to win people back to the truth.

⊕ talkabout

1. How easily are you taken in by appearances? Talk about an occasion when your first impressions of someone, based on their appearance, turned out to be quite wrong.

- How do we come to see the truth behind someone's misleading appearance?

⊕ investigate

In this session we will see that the struggles Timothy is facing as a church leader are part of a bigger picture. In these, the last days, he must hold on to what he knows is right.

⚫ Read 2 Timothy 3 v 1-9

2. The phrase "lovers of..." begins and finishes the list. Compare the two phrases. What is at the heart of the wrong attitudes described here?

3. These people have a form of godliness (they look godly), but deny its power (v 5). What is the power that they deny (compare 1 v 8)?

• What might these people look like in our churches today?

⊡ **getting personal**

Are you in danger of falling into any of the attitudes that Paul outlines in verses 2-5?

4. How do these people operate in their "ministry" (v 6-7)?

5. What comfort can Timothy take from the way Paul finishes this section of his letter in verses 8-9?

optional

⊡ **explore more**

In Acts 4 the apostles get their first taste of opposition since the birth of the church at Pentecost.

❯ **Read Acts 4 v 23-31**

What have these Christians understood about opposition to God's work? Having experienced persecution, what do they pray for? What is the result?

optional

⊡ **explore more**

Complete the following table—read the verses in the second column and discover how God's plan continued to prosper in spite of, or even because of, problems experienced by the church.

Problem for the church	What happened?
Christians lied to the Holy Spirit and God took their lives in judgment (Acts 5 v 1-10).	**Acts 5 v 11-14**
The apostles were imprisoned, flogged and banned from teaching about Jesus Christ (Acts 5 v 17-40).	**Acts 5 v 41 – 6 v 1**
A dispute between two groups in the church (Acts 6 v 1-6).	**Acts 6 v 7**
The death of Stephen at the hands of leading Jews, after preaching about Jesus Christ (Acts 8 v 54-60).	**Acts 8 v 1-4**

How do you usually feel when you hear about persecution, successful false teachers, disputes and discouragements in churches? In what way can you now respond differently?

⊕ investigate

> ❯ **Read 2 Timothy 3 v 10-17**

6. Timothy has worked with Paul and seen the way in which he goes about his gospel ministry. Contrast Paul with the people who have just been described (v 10-11).

> **DICTIONARY**
>
> **Imposters (v 13):** fakes; imposters.
> **Wise for (v 15):** knowledgeable about.
> **Rebuking (v 16):** telling someone they are making a mistake.

7. What sobering fact must Timothy face up to as he makes the choice to live a godly life (v 11-13)?

8. Timothy should continue with what he knows to be true (v 14, 15). What are the two reasons why he can stick confidently with this teaching?

➔ apply

9. Many people today believe that you can be a Christian without needing to belong to a church. Having read Paul's words here, how would you answer this from verses 10-15?

⊡ getting personal

How does verse 12 make you feel? Do you need to make more of your church—the teaching of Scripture (the Bible), and the example of godly Christians around you—to help you keep going in your faith?

⊻ investigate

10. Think about the four things that Scripture is useful for (v 16). Link these four uses of Scripture with instructions that Paul has already given Timothy.

 • Teaching:

 • Rebuking:

 • Correcting:

 • Training in righteousness:

 • How does using Scripture in these ways give Timothy a balanced ministry?

11. Surely Timothy knows Scripture is God-breathed. So why does he now need reminding of this, do you think?

⤇ apply

12. Are there any ways in which we should change the way we use Scripture in the light of these verses, both individually and as a church?

⬆ pray

As a group:

Thank God for those in your church who have been made wise for salvation through Scripture. Pray for those who use the Scripture to teach, rebuke, correct and train in righteousness, that through them, many may be thoroughly equipped for every good work.

On your own:

Ask God to help you to be truly godly and to demonstrate in your life His power—to endure and stick with the gospel. Thank Him for people like Paul, whose life and ministry encourage you to live a godly life in Christ Jesus.

▶ BEFORE NEXT TIME

- **READ AHEAD:** 2 Timothy 4

- **THINK AHEAD:** *How does this chapter sum up much of what Paul has been saying?*

7 2 Timothy 4
FINISHING THE RACE

The story so far

To guard the gospel we must be strong—not in our own strength, but in the grace that is in Jesus Christ.

Guarding the gospel means speaking out against false teaching. But this must be done gently, aiming to win people back to the truth.

Difficult times, because of the wrong attitudes of some in the church, are to be expected; we need to hold to the gospel message and gospel lifestyle.

⊕ talkabout

1. Forrest Gump said: "Life is like a box of chocolates—you never know what you're going to get!" Think of some popular images of life. How do you think these images may affect the way people live their lives?

We're going to see how Paul uses the images of a drink offering, a fight and a race to describe life as a Christian.

⊕ investigate

In this final chapter, we'll see Paul still encouraging Timothy in a way that sums up the message of the whole letter. Even the personal remarks at the end are not random comments—instead, they fit closely with the rest of the letter. So, as Paul gets ready to write what might be his last words to Timothy, he pauses, takes a deep breath and says...

▶ Read 2 Timothy 4 v 1-8

2. What is the long-term view that Timothy must keep in mind as he listens to Paul's final instructions (v 1)?

DICTIONARY

Doctrine (v 3): the study of who God is and how He relates to the world.
Evangelist (v 5): someone who tells non-believers the gospel.
Discharge (v 5): do what's required to do something.

- In what way is this both the greatest encouragement and the biggest warning that Timothy could have?

3. In contrast to the long-term view, the immediate situation facing Timothy is false teaching. In verses 3-4, what characteristic marks out false teaching and those who follow it?

➔ apply

4. How can these verses help us to choose which church leaders we should listen to?

⬇ investigate

5. List all of Paul's commands in verses 2 and 5. How will understanding both the long-term view (Question Two) and the immediate outlook (Question Three) help Timothy to carry out each of these instructions?

6. How do these verses sum up what Paul has been encouraging Timothy to do throughout the letter?

→ apply

7. What does it mean for us to be prepared to do these things "in season and out of season"?

⊡ getting personal

How often do you think about the long-term view—about the fact that you always stand in the presence of God and of Jesus Christ?

How often do you remember that Christ will return in glory, to judge the living and the dead, and to bring about His kingdom?

If people looked at the way you live, would they see that you are waiting for and looking forward to these things?

8. In verses 6 and 7, Paul uses three images of the Christian life in these verses. What are they? And how have they helped Paul to endure hardship and remain faithful to the Lord?

• v 6

• v 7a

• v 7b

9. How does Paul's situation make his commands even more important?

10. How will Paul's testimony here be an encouragement to Timothy?

▶ **Read 2 Timothy 4 v 9-22**

11. From these verses, pick out examples of:
• the way most people inside the church treated Paul:

• opposition from those outside the church:

• Paul's suffering for the gospel message:

• Paul's confidence in the Lord for the future:

➔ apply

In the end, Timothy has to make a choice between preaching the true gospel message that Paul proclaims (which brings opposition, desertion and suffering), and telling people what they want to hear (as many other teachers do). This is the choice for Christians in every generation—in the end, it's the choice for us too.

12. In what area of your life (as a church and as individual Christians) do you see the fiercest struggle taking place between "keeping the faith" (v 7) and "suiting your own desires" (v 3)?

13. Now that we have reached the end of 2 Timothy, what has been the biggest encouragement (or warning) for you to stay faithful to the true gospel?

⊡ explore more

Throughout this Bible-study series we have been investigating the last written words of the apostle Paul.

▶ **Read Revelation 22 v 12-21**

These are the last words of the Bible, written by the apostle John. John's last written words share similar concerns with those of Paul— Jesus Christ (who He is and what He will do when He returns), the Christian hope, and the problem of false teachers.

What does John say about these things?

How can we be encouraged by the "same mind" that Paul and John shared?

getting personal

If God were to demand your life tonight, could you make Paul's "last words" in verses 6-7 your own? If not, what do you need to change? And what can you do about that right now?

⬆ **pray**

Think about what you have learned from 2 Timothy, and turn those truths and challenges into prayer for...

• yourself

• people you know who are struggling to make the right choice

• your church leaders

• persecuted Christians around the world.

You may want to finish by restating John's prayer in Revelation 22 v 20—"Come, Lord Jesus".

Leader's Guide: 2 Timothy

INTRODUCTION

Leading a Bible study can be a bit like herding cats—everyone has a different idea of what the passage could be about, and a different line of enquiry that they want to pursue. But a good group leader is more than someone who just referees this kind of discussion. You will want to:

- correctly understand and handle the Bible passage. But also...

- encourage and train the people in your group to do this for themselves. Don't fall into the trap of spoon-feeding people by simply passing on the information in the Leader's Guide. Then...

- make sure that no Bible study is finished without everyone knowing how the passage is relevant for them. What changes do you all need to make in the light of the things you have been learning? And finally...

- encourage the group to turn all that has been learned and discussed into prayer.

Your Bible-study group is unique, and you are likely to know better than anyone the capabilities, backgrounds and circumstances of the people you are leading. That's why we've designed these guides with a number of optional features. If they're a quiet bunch, you might want to spend longer on talkabout. If your time is limited, you can choose to skip explore more, or get people to look at these questions at home. Can't get enough of Bible study? Well, some studies have optional extra homework projects. As leader, you can adapt and select the material to the needs of your particular group.

So what's in the Leader's Guide? The main thing that this Leader's Guide will help you to do is to understand the major teaching points in the passage you are studying, and how to apply them. As well as guidance on the questions, the Leader's Guide for each session contains the following important sections:

THE BIG IDEA

One key sentence will give you the main point of the session. This is what you should be aiming to have fixed in people's minds as they leave the Bible study. And it's the point you need to head back towards when the discussion goes off at a tangent.

SUMMARY

An overview of the passage, including plenty of useful historical background information.

OPTIONAL EXTRA

Usually this is an introductory activity that ties in with the main theme of the Bible study, and is designed to "break the ice" at the beginning of a session. Or it may be a "homework project" that people can tackle during the week.

So let's take a look at the various different features of a Good Book Guide:

⊕ talkabout

Each session kicks off with a discussion question, based on the group's opinions or experiences. It's designed to get people talking and thinking in a general way about the main subject of the Bible study.

⊥ investigate

The first thing you and your group need to know is what the Bible passage is about, which is the purpose of these questions. But watch out—people may come up with answers based on their experiences or teaching they have heard in the past, without referring to the passage at all. It's amazing how often we can get through a Bible study without actually looking at the Bible! If you're stuck for an answer, the Leader's Guide contains guidance on questions. These are the answers to direct your group to. This information isn't meant to be read out to people—ideally, you want them to discover these answers from the Bible for themselves. Sometimes there are optional follow-up questions (see ☑ in guidance on questions) to help you help your group get to the answer.

⊡ explore more

These questions generally point people to other relevant parts of the Bible. They are useful for helping your group to see how the passage fits into the "big picture" of the whole Bible. These sections are OPTIONAL—only use them if you have time. Remember that it's better to finish in good time having really grasped one big thing from the passage, than to try and cram everything in.

→ apply

We want to encourage you to spend more time working at application—too often, it is simply tacked on at the end. In the Good Book Guides, apply sections are mixed in with the investigate sections of the study. We hope that people will realise that application is not just an optional extra, but rather, the whole purpose of studying the

Bible. We do Bible study so that our lives can be changed by what we hear from God's word. If you skip the application, the Bible study hasn't achieved its purpose.

These questions draw out practical lessons that we can all learn from the Bible passage. You can review what has been learned so far, and think about practical differences that this should make in our churches and our lives. The group gets the opportunity to talk about what they personally have learned.

⊥ getting personal

These can be done at home, but it is well worth allowing a few moments of quiet reflection during the study for each person to think and pray about specific changes they need to make in their own lives. Why not have a time for reporting back at the beginning of the following session, so that everyone can be encouraged and challenged by one another to make application a priority?

⊤ pray

In Acts 4 v 25-30 the first Christians quoted Psalm 2 as they prayed in response to the persecution of the apostles by the Jewish religious leaders. Today however, it's not as common for Christians to base prayers on the truths of God's word as it once was. As a result, our prayers tend to be weak, superficial and self-centred rather than bold, visionary and God-centred.

The prayer section is based on what has been learned from the Bible passage. How different our prayer times would be if we were genuinely responding to what God has said to us through His word.

1

Overview
WHAT'S 2 TIM ALL ABOUT?

THE BIG IDEA

As the next generation of the church, our most important task is to guard the gospel from change, and pass it on to the following generation.

Note: This overview session, while helpful to orientate people towards the big themes of 2 Timothy, is not vital. All the material in it is dealt with in more detail in Sessions 2 – 7. If it suits your group to have fewer studies, feel free to start with Session Two.

SUMMARY

The aim of this session is to provide an overview of the background to 2 Timothy, and give people an opportunity to discover some of the big themes of the letter. Timothy was a younger Christian leader who had accompanied Paul on some of his missionary journeys (see Acts 16 v 1-5). Paul later sent him to help lead churches that Paul had started (eg: 1 Thessalonians 3 v 2; 1 Timothy 1 v 2-3). When Paul writes him this second letter, Timothy is probably still leading and teaching the church in Ephesus. Paul thinks very highly of Timothy (see Philippians 2 v 19-24). Paul, however, knows he himself is coming to the end of his time. So what are Paul's final instructions to Timothy and to those who have heard the gospel because of his ministry?

Paul's main concern is that, already, there is false teaching in the church—a situation that will continue into the future. The vital need of the hour, therefore, is to guard the gospel—not by locking it away where no one can get to it, but by teaching it faithfully to a new generation of Christians, and equipping them, in turn, to pass it on.

OPTIONAL EXTRA

You could extend Q1 by constructing a "last words" quiz as a fun activity to introduce the whole Bible-study course.

Alternatively, as a follow-up to Explore More, you could get people to write out a summary of the gospel for homework, or even challenge them to write an evangelistic leaflet. You will need to set aside some time next session for feedback and encouragement.

GUIDANCE ON QUESTIONS

1. If you could plan your last words, what would you like to say? The aim of this question is to help the group appreciate that 2 Timothy contains the last words of Paul to come down to us. It highlights the significance of last words in revealing what is ultimately important to the person who speaks them. You may need to get the ball rolling with your own ideas, or choose a few examples of the last words of famous people, which the group can discuss. Google "last words" to find plenty of examples. (See optional extra above.)

2. Read 2 Timothy 1 v 2-5. What does Paul think of Timothy now? v 2—Paul views Timothy as a dear son; v 3—Paul is always praying for him; v 4—Paul longs to see him; v 5—Paul is convinced that Timothy has true faith.

3. Read 1 v 15-17, 2 v 9 and 4 v 16. What is Paul's situation? 1 v 16-17; 2 v 9—Paul is in chains (ie: in prison) in Rome; 4 v 16; 1 v 15-17—he has already been on trial once, and because of this, many people have deserted him, although some have stood by him.

4. Read 2 v 17-18. What is the situation in the church? Some people are teaching things that are untrue; this is causing others to stop believing the truth about Jesus.

5. Read 3 v 13 and 4 v 3-4. What things are expected in the future? The false teaching that Timothy is facing is just a small example of what Paul expects generally. In fact, many people in the church like the false teaching because it tells them what they want to hear.

6. APPLY: If you were Paul, what sort of things might be going through your mind as you faced this situation? Let the group imagine how they might feel in Paul's shoes—despair? panic? self-pity? hopelessness?… or trying to trust God? Help your group to appreciate the shock that might be felt about the emergence of false teachers in the church. Remember that the church was still in its first generation; older members would have been alive at the time of Jesus' earthly ministry; they would still remember the world as it was in the "bad old days", before Jesus' sacrifice on the cross. Imagine then, what it would be like, not only to hear about teachers in the church denying these fantastic truths, but to hear that false teaching was going to be an ongoing problem, would be welcomed by some, and that through it, people would turn away from the gospel.

• **How similar are the problems facing the church today (both locally and worldwide)?** The aim of this follow-on question is to show that the issues raised in 2 Timothy are still very much with us today. Worldwide, many Christians are "in chains" for preaching the gospel. Open Doors International or www.barnabasfund. org have useful websites to investigate if you feel that your group would benefit from some information about the persecuted church worldwide. Similarly, you may want to briefly mention a couple of recent examples of false teaching that your group could be affected by.

• **What sort of things do you hope to learn from Paul as you study this letter?** This question is to encourage people to expect that they will be practically helped as they do these Bible studies.

7. Read 1 v 13-14. What is Paul's big concern? The two commands in 1 v 13-14 go alongside each other. "The pattern of sound teaching" and "the good deposit that was entrusted to you" both refer to the same thing—the gospel message about Jesus, and the implications that it has for our lives. This is what Paul and the other apostles taught, just as Jesus had told them to, and it is what Paul had passed on to Timothy. The two commands are quite similar, and each helps explain what the other means. The reason for keeping to "the pattern of sound teaching" is to guard "the good deposit" (gospel message): the way to guard the gospel is to "keep to the pattern of sound teaching". Paul's big concern is that Timothy will guard the gospel from being changed (for example, by the false teaching of the time), and that he will use this teaching as the pattern for his own ministry.

8. Read 2 v 2. What is Paul's plan for achieving this? Guarding the gospel message does not mean locking it away where no one can get to it! It does mean teaching it faithfully to a new generation, and so equipping that generation to pass it on again.

EXPLORE MORE

Read John 3 v 16. Try to construct an outline of the good news. What do these verses tell us about... God? ourselves? Jesus and His death? faith? the alternative? By answering the questions, your group will be able to go over the facts of the gospel several times and have plenty of opportunity to clear up misunderstandings.

- **God:** God is a God who loves the world He made; God sent Jesus to be a sacrifice to rescue sinners; Jesus' death shows us how great and deep God's love for us is, ie: He bears the punishment in Himself for people who deserve to perish; God is a Judge—the word "perish" sums up the truth that we are deserving of death.
- **Ourselves:** Because of the sin of which we are all guilty, we all fall short of the glory of God; we can do nothing to justify ourselves, but God justifies us in Jesus Christ as a gift of grace; we can't boast about being saved because we haven't done anything to make it possible; we need to give up trying to impress God with our "good" deeds, and instead, put our faith in what Jesus Christ has done, if we want to be justified.
- **Jesus and His death:** Jesus Christ can save us if we believe in Him; Jesus Christ can free us from our slavery to sin and death; Jesus Christ can turn away God's anger against us, and make it possible for us to be reconciled with God; God will declare us "not guilty" if we trust in Jesus.
- **Faith:** Good works do not make us right with God—it is God who makes sinners righteous, through faith in Jesus. Faith in Jesus is not just believing He lived and was God incarnate, but putting our trust in

His work on the cross to bring us to God, which involves letting go of trusting in our own good works or religion.

- **The alternative:** those outside of Christ will perish; this is the natural state of mankind, and it is why the gospel is so important, and why it must be guarded from corruption. Guarding the gospel is not just a matter of arguments over niggly details of doctrine or theology. It is life and death stuff. If we get it wrong, we perish. If we tell others a false gospel we will be complicit in their eternal damnation.

Now see if you can explain what the gospel is in your own words. Encourage your group to practise explaining this gospel message to each other simply and clearly.

9. Read 2 v 25-26. What else will Paul's plan involve for Timothy? As well as teaching positively, Timothy must also teach against false teachers in an attempt to correct them, though he must do this gently.

10. Read 1 v 8 and 3 v 12. What will happen to Timothy in the process? Paul tells Timothy to expect to suffer for the gospel because of persecution. This seems to be both because of opposition from outside the church, and from false teachers inside.

- **What is Paul worried that Timothy might do (1 v 8)?** It's clear from 1 v 8 that Paul is concerned that Timothy might become ashamed of the gospel (because of the pressures from both inside and outside the church), and also ashamed of Paul (because he is now locked up like a criminal).

11. APPLY: If you were Timothy, what sort of things might be going through your mind? Try to get the group to imagine themselves in Timothy's shoes. Would they be frightened? Overwhelmed by the task? Desperate to talk to Paul?

- **How similar are the experiences of Christians today (both locally and worldwide)?** Give your group the opportunity to share how they have felt on occasions when they have been ridiculed, rejected or intimidated because of their stand for Christ. Be prepared to get the ball rolling with some examples of your own. You could read out or print up excerpts from some testimonies (try the internet) of Christians who have suffered for their faith in other parts of the world. Try to find examples that give an insight into the fears and anxieties of these Christian brothers and sisters (see notes for Q6 above).

- **What sort of things do you hope to learn along with Timothy as you study this letter?** The aim of this question is to encourage people to expect that God can change them as they study together.

12. Read 1 v 9-10. What's the biggest encouragement to Timothy to still do his job? First make sure that everyone in the group understands what Timothy's job is—to preach the gospel message. This will be a difficult job, but the gospel is wonderful news that brings life through Christ and is all about the Lord who has saved us, not because of anything we have done but because of His grace.

PRAY

It is usual for groups to ask if anyone has any concerns or issues that the rest of the group can pray for. But often this means that the prayer time is crowded out with our problems. However you structure the prayer times in your group, try to ensure that adequate time is given to "praying in" the things we have discussed. It may be preferable to have a time to do this *before* asking people to "share for prayer".

If your group is unused to open prayer, then operate it as a "guided prayer" time at first until they become more confident. Say out loud some subjects for prayer, and leave a silence so that they can pray silently.

BEFORE NEXT TIME

Encourage the group to do the preparatory reading for next time.

2

2 Timothy 1 v 1-10

FANNING THE FLAME

THE BIG IDEA

Don't be ashamed of the gospel! We can and must stand up for it.

SUMMARY

This session looks at Paul's concerns for Timothy and how Paul encourages him in his God-given task of teaching and guarding the gospel. Although Timothy has always been

a faithful and reliable co-worker with Paul in gospel ministry, Paul is well aware of the pressures that Timothy faces, in particular, the temptation to be ashamed of the gospel and of Paul himself (v 8). Paul challenges Timothy to join with him in suffering for the gospel, but he gives this difficult challenge in the context of great encouragements. He reassures Timothy of his own great and prayerful love for him (v 3-4); he reminds him of how God has worked in his life in the past (v 5); he points out that God gives His people a spirit of power (v 7)—power to suffer for the gospel (v 8); he explains again to Timothy just how wonderful the gospel really is (v 9-10).

The purpose of this session is to make us aware of how we too can be tempted to be ashamed of the gospel, and of other Christians who boldly make a stand for Jesus Christ. We are challenged to face up to the fact that gospel ministry will involve suffering, but also to rediscover the wonder of the Christian message. The session also deals with common errors in the way we understand "God-given gifts" and "God's power" from the New Testament. There is an opportunity for everyone to reflect on whether they are truly saved, and for Christians to think about how to encourage others to keep on teaching the gospel.

OPTIONAL EXTRA

If you have a suitable location, you could get your group to try to light a small fire. Or you could show an excerpt about fire-lighting from a DVD of a survival expert (like Ray Mears). This activity relates to 1 v 6—to "fan into flame the gift of God".

Another suggestion relates to Q10. This is more suitable for established Christians and aims to impact them with the power of the gospel. Play a recording of a powerful gospel sermon. Eg: download an early Billy Graham sermon (try *Death* at sermonindex. net) or read an evangelistic sermon by C.H.Spurgeon, or the famous sermon of the Welsh preacher Christmas Evans, entitled *The World as a Graveyard*. Or excerpts from Jonathan Edwards' *Sinners in the Hand of an Angry God*. (You can download both the latter from www.thegoodbook.co.uk on the

page for this Good Book Guide). Although written in old-fashioned English, they have a graphic power detailing the appalling peril confronting everyone without the gospel, and the wonderful rescue that only the gospel can bring.

GUIDANCE ON QUESTIONS

1. Imagine you have a friend who is a Christian leader, and whose job is turning out to be a bit of a nightmare because of opposition from inside and outside the church. How might you try to encourage them? People may have practical suggestions. But the main focus of the question is to share ideas about what we can say to someone in this situation. There is a range of right answers to this opening question, but as the session progresses, it will be interesting to compare your group's ideas with what Paul says to encourage Timothy. You can return to this question at the end of the session (see last part of Q13).

2. When Paul sets aside time to pray for Timothy, what things come into his head (v 3-5)? When Paul prays for Timothy, what comes to his mind is thankfulness, longing to see Timothy, Timothy's tears (maybe on parting from Paul), and Timothy's sincere faith, which was taught to him by his faithful mother and grandmother. It must have been very difficult for Timothy to be separated from Paul. Clearly, he had worked with Paul for a long time. Now his mentor was suffering in prison, and he was alone.

3. Paul is about to give Timothy a challenge (v 6-8). What does Paul do first to encourage him? Point out the importance of the fact that Paul encourages Timothy before he challenges him. Challenges are necessary, as we shall see later in this letter. But we should never forget that the fifth fruit of the Spirit is kindness (Galatians 5 v 22).

- **verses 3-4:** Paul assures Timothy of his love and his prayers for him.
- **verse 5:** Paul reminds Timothy of how God has worked in his life through his mother and grandmother to bring him to "sincere faith". If God has already worked in Timothy's life so, He can do so again.

4. In verse 6, Paul challenges Timothy to keep using the gift of teaching and leadership that God has given him. What does this picture of fanning a flame tell us about Timothy's gift and what he needed to do? Many people think of a gift as enabling you to do something well without much thought or effort eg: a gift for comedy or for putting people at ease. But Paul tells Timothy that he needs to fan his gift into flame—Timothy needs to invest effort in using his gift. If appropriate, you could get your group to share any experiences they may have of lighting a fire—in some situations this can be a tricky procedure involving a lot of concentrated attention and energy. (Also see Optional Extra on previous page).

Timothy is in danger of becoming timid and so not using his God-given gift. **Note:** Christopher Green, writing in *Finishing the Race: Reading 2 Timothy Today*, comments that "cowardice" (see NRSV) is a much better translation than "timidity" because, he says: "Paul is not criticising Timothy's personality, but identifying the danger that Timothy will, at a critical moment, drop out of the responsibilities of Christian leadership because the personal cost will be too high."

5. What powerful reason does Paul give Timothy to work at using his God-given gift (v 7)? God has given Timothy a spirit of power, of love and of self-discipline

(v 7)—presumably this refers to the Holy Spirit. In other words, God is at work in him and so he shouldn't be cowardly and give up on the job of teaching God's truth, no matter how hard it is. This is linked with what Paul says in v 5—there is evidence that God has been very much at work in Timothy's life before, so Timothy can have confidence that God will continue.

⌄

- **What will Timothy be able to do with the three things mentioned in verse 7 that God's Spirit can give him: power, love and self discipline?** God's Spirit can give him the power to keep using his gift (see also v 8b, which is covered in Q7), the love he needs to love those who oppose him, and the self-discipline he needs not to give up.

6. Why might Timothy be "ashamed" of the gospel? It is easy to become ashamed of the gospel message when others around us not only refuse to accept it, but pour scorn on it. For Timothy, there was the added embarrassment that the most famous teacher of the gospel, the apostle Paul, was now locked up in a Roman prison and appeared to be simply a common criminal.

- **Why is being ashamed of Paul so close to being ashamed of the gospel, do you think?** Paul is a true gospel teacher, proclaiming the gospel as God told him to do, so to be ashamed of what he does is really being ashamed of what he says, which is the gospel.

⌄

- **In what way can Christians today still be ashamed of the apostle Paul?** Paul is wrongly blamed for making Christianity anti-women and homophobic, and for substituting his own "hard-line" teaching in place of the "true" teaching of Jesus Christ. It may be helpful for people to share experiences of occasions when they have come across these kinds of attitudes, and for the group to discuss how to respond.

7. What sort of power does God offer to overcome this shame, according to verse 8? God offers us the power to suffer for the gospel ie: strength to keep teaching and sharing the gospel message, whatever the opposition.

8. APPLY: What things can tempt us to be ashamed of the gospel (or of true gospel teachers)? Allow people to make suggestions based on their own experience of being a Christian. It's likely that people will mention one or more of the following: when others seem to disagree with the gospel (even others inside the church); when the gospel is likely to get us into trouble (with friends, family, employers, the press, even the law); when other people get into trouble for preaching the gospel, or speak out for it despite opposition.

9. APPLY: How does Paul's understanding of "the power of God" (v 8b) differ from that of many people today? Many think the power of God is only seen when difficult situations are changed in a wonderful or miraculous way to bring relief from suffering and hardship. Paul, however, uses the term "the power of God" to mean that God helps Christians to keep going in their difficult circumstances. In other words, when Christians keep going in the faith in spite of their suffering, that's when we can see the power of God at work.
Note: It can be liberating for people to free

their thinking about God's power from only expecting signs and wonders and miracles. When we understand that the weak and shameful foolishness of the cross was God's greatest act of power, we will begin to appreciate better how our perseverance through suffering also shows the power of God. Then we can stop waiting for miracles and instead, get on with the work of the gospel, just as Paul did.

EXPLORE MORE
Read John 12 v 23-33. What event is Jesus talking about here? His death on a cross, which is about to take place in the next few days (v 24 and 32-33).
What does Jesus say to show that this event would mean shame and suffering for Him? We know Jesus expected to suffer great pain and shame because He was troubled at what awaited Him; He mentions that a normal response would be to cry out to His Father to save Him (v 27). He describes His death as being "lifted up from the earth" ie: it would be public and therefore very humiliating (v 32-33).
How would it show the power of God? Through this shameful death, both the Son of Man (v 23) and the Father (v 28) would be glorified; the prince of this world (the devil) would be driven out (v 31); and Jesus would draw all men to Himself (v 32).
What does Jesus say about His followers here? Verses 25-26: Those who give their lives to Him will have life eternally; whoever serves Him will one day be with Him.

10. Read verses 9-10. Why are the Lord and His gospel worth suffering for? This question will challenge the group to be powerfully motivated by the gospel—these are not sterile facts, but life- and eternity-changing truth. The Lord and His gospel are uniquely wonderful: God has saved us "not because of anything we have done, but because of his own purpose and grace" (v 9); we are called to a holy life (v 9)—with God's help, we can turn our backs on all the sin and selfishness that has ruined God's creation; Jesus Christ has destroyed death and replaced it with life and immortality for those who trust in His gospel. Let people pick out the things that strike them most. If the discussion seems a little flat (because the answers are obvious and people are already familiar with these truths), you could get your group to work out what is the reality for those without the gospel, by identifying the opposite of the points mentioned in verses 9-10, or discussing the extra question that follows. (See also optional extra below.)

⌄

• **What difference did these truths make to your life when you first became a Christian?**

11. APPLY: Can you explain what God has done for you in Jesus Christ? Why not have a go, using v 9-10? This question aims to help those who are not used to talking about the gospel, and those who would like to share the good news but don't know what to say. Although your group may already have tried this, as with any activity, practice will make it easier. People could talk about being saved from sins (v 9), or becoming aware that, in Jesus, it's possible to live a different sort of life ("called us to a holy life"—v 9), or knowing that they have life and immortality through Jesus (v 10), or discovering that God is a God of grace—that we can't earn any of this, but it is freely given in Jesus Christ (v 9-10).

12. APPLY: How can we avoid being ashamed, and instead, carry out God's

command to pass on His message to others? There might be lots of ideas, but an important one is to understand the gospel better so we see how wonderful it is, and realise all the more what God has done for us. Allow people to share what has struck them from this passage. Have a suggestion of your own to get discussion started.

13. APPLY: How can we encourage our church leaders not to give up on this task? Our leaders will be under similar pressures to Timothy. Try to come up with some practical suggestions—these should also include putting a stop to those things that will discourage our leaders. Eg: Tell them, or write a note of thanks, when you have been encouraged by the teaching. Let your leader know when something they taught has been useful in a conversation, when you have put into something into practice, or have understood for the first time something that confused you. Ask questions about Christian teaching and things that you read in the Bible. Avoid looking bored or impatient during teaching, and be responsive to what is said.
Look again at your answers to Q1. Would you make any changes to the way in which you go about encouraging "your friend"? It may be that people's answers will have changed significantly since the beginning of the session. Or they may now have some idea of what to say where previously they had none. People can mention that God has been at work in their friend's life (v 4), that He gives power to suffer for the gospel (v 7-8) and that the Lord is bringing people life through the gospel (v 9-10).

3 2 Timothy 1 v 11-18
GUARDING THE GOSPEL

THE BIG IDEA

We must guard the gospel by teaching it, as Paul did, and by supporting gospel teachers, as Onesiphorus did, regardless of suffering and shame.

SUMMARY

This session brings us to Paul's great concern for the future of the church, and his main challenge to Timothy. In the middle of concerted encouragements to "not be ashamed", Paul tells Timothy to keep on teaching what he has heard from Paul and to guard the gospel message (1 v 13-14).

In these verses, Paul shares his own experience of being a gospel teacher. He has been appointed by God to this task (v 11), and yet, he summarises his experience as one of suffering (v 12)—in fact, it is precisely because of his task that he is suffering (v 12—"That is why I am suffering"). He is not only chained in prison, but has been deserted by nearly every other believer (v 15). Only Onesiphorus has not been ashamed of him and has given him practical help. And yet, Paul can be positive about his experience because he trusts God, and knows that on the final day of Christ's return, he will not have slogged and suffered in vain (v 12).

In a strange way, Timothy (and we) can be encouraged by Paul's experiences. The contrast between Paul and Timothy shows that it is not our circumstances (which we cannot change) that make us cowardly or ashamed. Rather, it is the question of whether or not we trust God—this is something that we can learn to do, especially when we are encouraged by the example of fellow Christians, like Paul and Onesiphorus.

Paul also sets out the task for which Timothy has been appointed—his big command is sandwiched between the encouraging examples of Paul himself, and of Onesiphorus. Paul tells Timothy to keep teaching what he has heard Paul teach (v 13). This is the way in which the gospel will be guarded for the next generation of Christians (v 14). This is not something Timothy has to do alone—as well as the examples of Paul and Onesiphorus, he also has the help of the Holy Spirit.

This session looks at why the church today still needs to follow Paul's big command, why churches sometimes fail to do this, and how we can try to make sure that this is what will happen in our own churches. Christians are challenged to ask themselves how well they know the gospel, and how important Paul's big command is to them.

OPTIONAL EXTRA

After the study, lead a discussion on how your group could set up an "Onesiphorus project" ie: a project to give practical help to a Christian leader or church that is suffering for the Christian faith—either locally or abroad. This may involve raising money, sending letters or parcels, campaigning on their behalf, or organising and sending practical assistance. What your group does will depend on the contacts and characters within your group. The important thing is to link your project to what has been learned from the example of Onesiphorus, a Christian brother who was not ashamed to support gospel work in what was perceived to be a shameful situation.

GUIDANCE ON QUESTIONS

1. What do you think is the most important job of the church? Share some of the different ideas that you have come across, both inside and outside the church. Depending on the maturity of your group, there may be several different answers to this question. Some people may feel that you cannot single out any one job that is most important—many aspects of the work of churches are inter-related eg: Bible-teaching and evangelism. However, don't allow the group to get hung up on the phrase "the most important job", which is simply used as a way of getting people to think about what must be a priority for church ministry.

It's not important for people to get the correct answer at this stage, because the purpose of the question is to highlight the fact that there are many jobs that people expect churches to give priority to, from pastoral care of church members to stopping the moral rot in our nation, to building a more just and equal society, to saving the planet from ecological disaster. As you go through this session, it should become clear that Paul's priority is to see that the next generation of Christian leaders (such as Timothy) guard the gospel.

2. What was Paul's own experience of being a gospel teacher? Paul was appointed by God to be a gospel preacher (v 11); he has suffered for doing this (v 12); has been deserted by others (v 15), and imprisoned (v 16—though Onesiphorus has stood by him); yet he is not ashamed (v 12).

3. How can he be so positive about his experience, despite the circumstances? Verse 12b—Paul knows that God can guard him and his ministry, and keep them safe until the day of Jesus' return, whatever other people might do to him.

4. Why does Paul describe his difficult experiences as a gospel teacher, do you think? Point out that Paul has already actually suffered (and is still suffering now) the kinds of things that Timothy is merely worried about. Yet Paul is not ashamed, whereas, as we saw last session, Timothy is clearly in danger of becoming ashamed both of the gospel and of Paul. Paul is not ashamed, because he is trusting God. Surely Timothy, who is not yet in chains, can follow his example. You can use the following optional extra questions to help your group work this out for themselves:

- **Contrast Paul and Timothy. How have they suffered as gospel teachers?** Paul—a great deal; Timothy—as far as we know, not yet.
- **Are they in danger of being ashamed of the gospel?** Paul—not at all; Timothy—in enough danger to spur Paul to write this letter to him.
- **What explains the difference between them?** Paul trusts God (v 12).
- **Is it suffering and opposition that makes us ashamed of the gospel—or something else?** It's not our difficult circumstances that make us ashamed of the gospel, but our lack of trust in God, which means we are influenced more by what the world thinks and says than what God thinks and says.
- **Why is this good news for Christians who are tempted to be ashamed?** We can't change our circumstances, but with the Spirit's help we can change our thinking and learn to listen to and trust God.

EXPLORE MORE

Read 2 Cor 11 v 24-33. How might Paul have been tempted to respond to these painful experiences? Paul could have been tempted to feel proud of himself and his ability to survive. He could have got angry and vengeful with those who caused him trouble eg: false brothers. He could have got angry with God, who had allowed these things to happen to him, or he could have started to think that God wasn't able or willing to look after him. He could have given in to cowardice, intimidation or discouragement; he could have been tempted to tone down his ministry or give it up altogether.

See also 2 Cor 4 v 17-18. What kept Paul going through weakness and suffering? Paul's suffering had a great purpose. Paul knew that as people looked at him they would see a weak man in whom the life and power of Jesus were at work, and this could bring them the life of Jesus as well (4 v 11-12) ie: others would become Christians through seeing Paul's weakness and sufferings. Paul looked forward to more and more people becoming Christians, leading to increasing glory to God (4 v 15). But Paul also had a great hope in his suffering. He knew that one day God would raise him to eternal life, just as He had raised Jesus Christ, and that in eternity he would be compensated immeasurably for everything he had suffered in this world (see 4 v 14, 17-18).

How might this encourage us, when we feel weak during times of hardship?

5. Look at verse 13. What does Timothy need to do if he is to keep the pattern of sound teaching? "What you heard from me…" (v 13). He needs to know and remember the gospel teaching that Paul has passed on to him.

6. Look at verse 14. What does Timothy need if he is to "guard the good deposit"? "With the help of the Holy Spirit who lives in us" (v 14).

- **Why is that essential, do you think?** Without the Holy Spirit, Timothy would simply give in to the pressures around him and change or water down the teaching of the gospel. Guarding the gospel is an impossible task in his own strength.

7. Put Paul's big command in verses 13-14 into your own words. You could let people work on this in twos and threes, or individually if they prefer. Provide some spare sheets of paper so that people can try out a couple of drafts. Or you may feel that people would find this easier if they had longer to think about it at home. Sometimes people are more willing to share something that they have thought about at length and have then written down.

8. APPLY: Which parts of the gospel do we especially need to guard, because they are under threat today? First allow people to come up with suggestions. Threats that we can see today include the following:

- The idea that humans are basically good is popular, with the result that many are unwilling to accept human sinfulness.
- The teaching that when Jesus died on the cross, He was being punished by God (substitutionary atonement) is under attack from some church leaders today.
- The truth that Jesus is the only way to God is very unpopular in our multi-faith society.
- The standards of holiness that the NT expects to see in the lives of Christians are constantly under pressure to be downgraded—social trends such as divorce, sex before marriage, homosexual practice and euthanasia are now accepted

by many Christians as inevitable and even permissible.

9. APPLY: Why do you think that many churches have given up teaching the gospel like this? There are a number of reasons why churches may have given up on "sound teaching". Here are a few of the possible reasons, which you can share with your group if they need help in answering this question:

- Many people believe that word-based communication is no longer effective because we live in a "visual" culture that is dominated by images;
- There are now (as there always have been) many alternative activities and strategies that compete for the energy and resources of churches, such as charitable and community work, ethical debates and political campaigns. None of these in themselves is bad, but when they start to dominate the agenda, they remove gospel proclamation from its central position.
- In a post-Christian society many of the teachings of the gospel are seen as politically incorrect, irrelevant or "disproved" by science—church ministry is affected by this cultural pressure.
- **What could you say to those who believe that Paul's big command is no longer relevant or practical in our modern culture?** Paul's big command is still relevant today because it's the only way the gospel message will survive, and the gospel is not just any old message. Unlike all the other messages communicated in our society, the gospel is the power of God for the salvation of everyone who believes (Romans 1 v 16)—it is uniquely powerful and uniquely important. Without the gospel there will be no church, so the survival of the gospel

from generation to generation must be the priority of the church.

10. APPLY: How can we make sure that the pattern of Paul's teaching is kept by young Christians in our own church and by ourselves? Make sure that everyone understands how the two instructions in verses 13-14 are linked. The way to guard the gospel is to teach it, as Paul taught it—not to lock it away where no one can get to it. Encourage your group to share lots of ideas. You may wish to mention some of the following:

- We need to hear the gospel in our church meetings. What do our church leaders talk about in their teaching sessions? Do people who come to our meetings get regular opportunities to learn how and why Jesus Christ alone can save them from their sins, and where this teaching comes from in the Bible?
- Our churches need to teach new Christians (or Christians who aren't confident about the teaching of the gospel). Are there discipleship courses or small-group Bible studies for people like this?
- More mature Christians should be talking to newer Christians about Bible teaching— and watching out for wrong ideas. What about meeting one-to-one with a younger Christian for Bible-reading, encouragement and prayer? What about making sure you discuss the Bible teaching with Christians that you get into conversation with after a church meeting.
- Bible-based Christian newspapers and magazines can be a good way to find out about ideas in our society that threaten the gospel eg: *Evangelicals Now* (a monthly newspaper); *The Briefing* (a monthly magazine). These could be made available from a church bookstall.

11. How did Onesiphorus show that he was not ashamed of Paul (v 16-17)? Onesiphorus searched all the prisons in Rome until he found Paul, and then refreshed him (ie: brought him food etc). In other words, he stood by him and gave practical help, despite the shamefulness of Paul's situation. Help your group to imagine what it must have been like to search for Paul—the horrible places that Onesiphorus must have visited (think how grim and intimidating prisons can be even today); the callous, contemptuous officials that he would have to deal with; the humiliations that he might have to go through, first to get information, and then to get permission to see Paul (endless queues, flat refusals, demands for bribes, strip-searches); the people he had to mix with, and would be identified with, on his visits to prison and to prison officials (the "criminal underclass" that everyone else despised).

- **Why would Onesiphorus' example be a big challenge to Timothy?** Paul mentions that Onesiphorus "was not ashamed of my chains" (v 16), in direct contrast to his concern that Timothy might be tempted to be ashamed of him (v 8).

12. APPLY: How can we follow the example of Onesiphorus today? There are two aspects to this question:

- When might we be called not to be ashamed of those suffering because they stand up for the gospel? Maybe people can think of small as well as big examples eg: standing by fellow Christians when others are speaking against them, supporting your church leader when he has made a stand for something the Bible teaches and is under fire from people in the community, etc.
- What practical help can we give to Christians who are suffering for standing up for the gospel? Don't forget to mention Christians in other countries—often they suffer many practical hardships as a result of persecution. For more information about how Christians in the west can help, go to www.barnabasfund.org

2 Timothy 2 v 1-13

4 ENDURING HARDSHIP

THE BIG IDEA

To guard the gospel we must be strong—not in our own strength, but in the grace that is in Jesus Christ.

SUMMARY

In 2 v 1-13 Paul sets out the challenges and the encouragements that Timothy will need to face intimidating opposition and hostility, and to put Paul's plan for the gospel into

action. Timothy will have to be strong, but Paul doesn't expect him to work up strength from his own character—he needs to look to Jesus Christ for this strength (2 v 1). Paul wants Timothy to carry out his bold plan with a bold attitude. Like a soldier, he needs to give up his own interests to focus on the job in hand and make sure that he pleases his commanding officer (2 v 3-4). Like an athlete, he needs to do things the right way, which may involve more hardship and slog, rather than by cheating (2 v 5). Like a farmer, he needs to work hard now so that in the future he can enjoy a share of the harvest (2 v 6).

Timothy can be encouraged by remembering who Jesus Christ is—His power, His own sufferings, and His utter faithfulness to all His promises (2 v 8, 13). He can also be encouraged by the knowledge that no one can stop God's word working to save God's people (2 v 9-10). With Christ, he doesn't need to fear death (2 v 11), nor that a life of suffering and hardship will be a wasted life (2 v 12). Finally though, he should be challenged by the stark warning (2 v 13) that if we disown Christ (ie: not endure), He will disown us.

This session challenges people to think about how to get involved with, or support, Paul's great plan for passing on the gospel in their own churches. People are also encouraged to share ways we can help one another with the same encouragements that Paul uses here to motivate Timothy. There is an opportunity to reflect on how we are most tempted to opt out of enduring hardship in the task of telling others the gospel, and to think about what will encourage us most to remain faithful to the end.

OPTIONAL EXTRA

After Q1, play an excerpt from a film or TV series of your choice that shows either a soldier preparing for a battle, or an athlete/sportsman in training, or a farmer clearing ground/ploughing/planting/weeding. The clip should give some idea of the hard work and physical discomfort involved.

GUIDANCE ON QUESTIONS

1. Share any experiences you may have had of being a soldier, an athlete, or a farmer. Or talk about what you have learned from the experiences of others—from family or friends, from films or from TV or radio programmes. What do these three roles have in common? This question is to prepare people for the characters (the soldier, the athlete and the hard-working farmer) that Paul uses in verses 5-6 to describe how we are to live the Christian life. Each role involves hard work and requires endurance. Help your group to imagine the sheer slog that is required for much of the time in each of these occupations. (See Optional Extra above.)

• **What keeps people going in each of these demanding professions?** The hope of a future reward. For the soldier—the battle won; for the athlete—winning the competition; for the farmer—a good harvest.

2. What is Paul's next instruction to Timothy in verse 1? To be strong.

• **Where is Timothy to find this?** He is to be "strong in the grace that is in Christ Jesus" (v 1). "In Christ Jesus": He doesn't have to look for strength in himself; rather, he needs to trust that Jesus Christ will give him the strength that is needed to guard the gospel and not be ashamed of it. "Strong in … grace": This is a gift of grace from Jesus—he doesn't deserve it—so no matter how cowardly and ashamed he has been, Jesus can still make him strong.

• **Why might this be just what Timothy needs to hear?** If Timothy does feel like giving up, he needs to hear the challenge to be strong. If he is feeling weak and unable to cope, there is the reminder that this strength comes from Jesus Christ—not from him.

3. In verse 2, Paul tells Timothy his plan for passing on the gospel message. What are the different links in the chain? Paul has taught Timothy; Timothy is to teach "reliable men" who are "qualified to teach"; these people are to teach others.

4. Why is this a bold plan in the circumstances? The reason that Paul has been put in prison is for teaching the gospel. And the reason that Timothy feels under pressure is that he has seen how teaching the gospel leads to suffering. Normally we would expect people to go quiet and keep their heads down in this sort of situation. But Paul shows bold thinking by planning for the gospel to go forward at a time when Christian leaders are under pressure, and when more gospel teaching may well lead to further opposition.

5. APPLY: What should we be doing as a church to make sure there is a next generation of faithful teachers who are able to pass God's message on? Give some practical examples. This is an opportunity for people to share ideas for training, or being trained ourselves, and training others to do this job. Suggestions could include the following:
- Do an evangelistic course or Bible study, aiming both to learn how to present the gospel, and to become familiar enough with the material to do it with someone who needs to learn the gospel message.
- Do a one-to-one Bible study with a more mature Christian who is able to teach, and then do the same Bible study with a less mature Christian who needs teaching.
- Organise a group in your church to do a Bible correspondence course together.
- Ask your leaders to put on occasional but regular training meetings that deal with evangelistic issues and major Christian

doctrines.
- All agree to read a Christian book, watch a DVD of a Christian speaker or hear a talk, and then meet together again to talk about what you have learned;
- Ask to get involved as a helper or trainee in a teaching ministry in your church (Sunday school, youth work, school CUs and Bible clubs, discipleship group, street evangelism, evangelistic courses, women's Bible study, men's breakfasts, etc).

6. What can Timothy learn from... Try to get the group to think about the things Paul points to in his description of these characters, rather than how they might be examples in other ways that these verses don't deal with. It may help us get Paul's point if we think of the opposites—a soldier who wants to go shopping on the day of battle, a cheating athlete, and a lazy farmer.

- **a soldier (v 3-4)?** The soldier teaches us to be ready to endure (rather than be cowardly), and to concentrate on the job in hand (rather than running away to do other things). The soldier's motivation is to please his commanding officer. So Timothy must get on with teaching the gospel and think of how to please Jesus Christ.

- **an athlete (v 5)?** The athlete teaches us to obey the rules of the sport (rather than cheat). So Timothy must do his job of teaching God's message in the way that God would want (ie: not distort it, or water it down to make it more attractive, or try to con people into believing it, or try to use it for his own personal gain, etc).

- **a hardworking farmer (v 6)?** The emphasis here is on "hardworking". A lazy farmer will end up with no crops. Teaching God's message is equally hard work, and Timothy must not give in to the temptation to be lazy.

7. What three encouragements in v 8, 9 and 10 does Paul give Timothy to persevere despite the difficult circumstances?

- **v 8:** Paul wants Timothy to remember who Jesus is. He is both the Messiah King "descended from [king] David" AND the one who conquered death. Both of these facts point to His power and also to the fulfilment of God's promises. Christ is all-powerful and God is completely faithful, so be encouraged.

Note: Verse 8 also implies Jesus had to suffer before He was raised from death— Paul and Timothy are just following in His footsteps.

- **v 9:** God's word is powerful—they can chain the messenger but they can't chain the message! Preaching the gospel will bring results, so be encouraged.

- **v 10:** Those God has chosen ("the elect") will get eternal salvation—God will make sure of it. It is worth suffering to make sure that people hear the gospel, because success is guaranteed, so be encouraged.

Note: It is interesting to note how Paul was affected by understanding the Bible teaching of "election" (the fact that God has already chosen His people, ie: who will be saved). It inspired and motivated Paul to suffer for the gospel and make sure that these chosen people would hear it.

By contrast, often when people hear this teaching, their reaction is one of "Why bother to teach the gospel at all?" since the destiny of everyone is already decided. They fail to understand that God has not only chosen who will be saved, but also how they will be saved—through Christians teaching the gospel message. Paul is a great example of how a true understanding of God's election will motivate us to teach and suffer for the gospel, not keep it quiet.

Some Christians find it difficult to believe that God chooses to save some people and not others (as stated in v 10), because this seems unfair to them. It may be helpful to spend some time on this issue after the session or arrange another time for this. For a brief yet biblical response, see the chapter entitled "Election" in *Bitesize Theology* by Peter Jeffery, published by Evangelical Press. Or refer to a good systematic theology eg: Chapter 32 of *Systematic Theology* by Wayne Grudem, published by IVP.

8. What fear is addressed by the encouragement in verse 11? Fear of dying. It is not unusual for Christians to fear death—it is the ultimate test of whether it is worthwhile to put our trust in the gospel. At the time of this letter, some of the false teachers who were a problem in the church at that time were questioning the resurrection (2 v 18). Similarly, we live in an age where it is commonplace to ridicule the resurrection—even professing Christians may discount the idea of a physical resurrection of the body. But Paul was prepared to invest his whole life for the gospel on the basis that Jesus Christ completely transforms the experience of death in His people (see also 1 Corinthians 15 v 14-24).

Christians no longer need to fear dying. If a Christian "died with him" (v 12)—ie: trusting in Christ and the gospel—they are guaranteed to live with Him. What we should fear is not death, but giving up our faith in Christ and the gospel.

9. What fear is addressed by the encouragement in verse 12a? Fear of enduring a life of hardship and suffering, only to discover in the end that our life has been wasted. But if we endure, whatever the pressures and sufferings, we will reign with Christ, and receive things more wonderful than any of those that we missed out on in this world (see Romans 8 v 18).

10. What warning is given in verse 12b?
It's very stark—if we give up on Jesus and the gospel, we will lose out on everything that He can do for His people. This should provoke the response: how can I make sure that I don't disown the Lord? The answer is what Paul has been telling Timothy (and us) all along—we need to endure in living to please Jesus Christ, running the race and working for the harvest.

11. Is verse 13 a warning or an encouragement?
Both! It is encouraging to know that Christ will always remain faithful and cannot disown Himself, as long as we endure and end up dying "with Him". It is an encouragement because we know His promise of salvation and eternal glory will be fulfilled—nothing can prevent this.
But this same truth is a terrible warning if we are faithless (ie: if we have disowned Him), because we also know that nothing can prevent His promise of judgment on those who have "not believed in the name of God's one and only Son" (John 3 v 18).

- **What is the difference between being "faithless" and having "little" or "weak" faith?** To be faithless is to have no faith at all. This describes someone who refuses to trust Christ—here, refusing to trust that a life of hardship and suffering now will be more than compensated by living and reigning with Christ in glory. It is important people understand the difference between a faithless person and one whose faith is weak. We may all sometimes give in to cowardice or shame. In these situations we need to repent and be encouraged again to "be strong in the grace that is in Christ Jesus". But a faithless person is someone who ends up

disowning Christ, probably in response to difficult personal experiences, and whose life takes a new, tragic direction away from the gospel. We should be aware that people who end up like this don't necessarily take a conscious decision to disown Christ. "Their attitude is probably more indicative of a direction in life than a momentary giving way to pressure, one weakness leading on to a further weakness, and an action becoming a cast of mind" (Christopher Green, *Finishing the Race*). This shows how important it is to heed the warning in v 13 every time we feel under pressure to give up.

EXPLORE MORE
How do these passages make you feel?
- **John 11 v 25-26:** Jesus is speaking about the fact that Christians will die physically, but what comes to a Christian after death is eternal life, so we will live even though we die. However, Jesus also says that Christians won't die ie: we won't really experience death, which means to be under God's judgment.
- **1 Corinthians 15 v 20-28:** Christ has already been raised from the dead as the firstfruits of His victory over death. When He comes again, those who belong to Him will also be physically raised from the dead, and then the end will come, when all enemies of God will be destroyed and He will be seen to rule over everything.
- **Revelation 22 v 3-5:** Christians will live in the wonderful presence of God and Jesus Christ in a perfect new creation, over which they will reign for ever.

These are tremendous truths—make sure Christians in your group understand that this is their future, so that they will be wonderfully encouraged to endure.

12. APPLY: When we meet together

with our church, what could we do to help other Christians receive the same encouragements and warnings that Paul gives to Timothy? How could we remind each other of...
- who Jesus is?
- the power of God's word?
- the guaranteed success of the gospel?
- the future of eternal glory?
- the terrible consequences of giving up on Jesus and the gospel?

This is an opportunity for people to share ideas for ways in which we can remind ourselves of the things that Paul wants us to be encouraged by. Our problem may be that because we know so much of what the Bible teaches about Jesus, it fails to impact us any longer. Or it could be that we know practically nothing eg: about how God is

working in other parts of the world, or how He has worked in the lives of the Christians around us. Here are a few suggestions: before you sing, saying together the words of a song that describes who Jesus is or what eternity will be like—it makes you think more about the words; reading out a relevant passage from a helpful Christian book; in pairs or small groups writing together a prayer that thanks God for who Jesus is, and then praying it; reading letters or testimonies from missionaries and Christians in other parts of the world, about what God is doing there (use personal contacts, visitors, mission organisations or the internet to get information); interviewing members of your church to find out what God has done in their lives; etc.

5 2 Timothy 2 v 14-26
CORRECTLY HANDLING THE WORD OF TRUTH

THE BIG IDEA
Guarding the gospel means speaking out against false teaching. But this must be done gently, aiming to win people back to the truth.

SUMMARY
Paul has instructed Timothy to guard the gospel by teaching faithfully what he himself had learned from Paul. But in the church where Timothy is a leader, there are people who are teaching differently. In particular, they are saying that the resurrection (of Christians—not Jesus) has already taken place (v 18). Paul is in no doubt that such teaching is deadly to Christian faith

(v 18)—he describes it as "gangrene" (v 17) and "the trap of the devil" (v 26). Paul gives Timothy very practical instructions on how to oppose such teaching.

The key point is that Timothy must correctly handle the word of truth himself (v 15). As a teacher of the word of truth, Timothy needs to discern between matters of fundamental importance and worthless quarrels—he must not hesitate to confront false teaching (v 25-26), but he must avoid stupid and foolish arguments (v 23), and warn those involved about their ungodliness (v 14).

Paul is aware that Timothy may be tempted in this situation in two ways. First, he may want to give in to false teaching—so

Paul challenges him to turn away from wickedness (v 19), and to cleanse himself [from false teaching] (v 21) so that he will be useful to his Master, the Lord Jesus. Alternatively, he may be tempted to react in an immature way to those who spread false teaching. Paul tells him to gently instruct those who oppose him (v 25), showing kindness and not giving in to resentment (v 24). The aim is not to win an argument, but to see those who have been deceived by the devil brought to repentance and a knowledge of the truth (v 25).

This session aims to help people see the serious consequences of false teaching and to think about what false teachings could threaten our faith today. People will be given some insight into the responsibilities of being a godly church leader, and there is an opportunity to discuss how all Christians can support their leaders in taking a stand against false teaching and "problem people" in the church. The session ends with a detailed case-study (see Optional Extra, p70).

GUIDANCE ON QUESTIONS

1. How do you feel and how do you react when people say things that you disagree with? The purpose of this question is to get people to think about their own responses to disagreements. The question is very general—the follow-up below focuses it specifically on Christian teaching. One of the issues highlighted in this session is various inappropriate responses to false teaching that Paul wants Timothy to avoid. It is helpful for people to think about the tendencies of their own personalities so that they can look out for those warnings that are particularly applicable to them. How people feel and react to disagreement will also depend on what is being disputed.

- Feelings: These will range from outrage, through concern, to indifference.
- Reactions: People tend to respond either confidently (confrontation, even anger) or unconfidently (unsure of what to say or think). Or, because they have no strong opinion, they simply ignore it.

- **How do you feel and react when people who call themselves Christians say things that seem to go against the Bible's teaching?**

2. Try to build up a picture of the problems that were facing the church where Timothy was a leader.
- **v 16-18:** False teaching from people inside the church eg: teaching that the resurrection has already taken place.
- **v 14 and 23:** arguments over things that it was not worth arguing about.
- **v 25:** opposition to leaders like Timothy.

3. Find words or phrases that Paul uses to describe this false teaching (see v 17 and 26).
- **v 17:** Paul describes this false teaching as "gangrene"—if untreated, it will spread and will be deadly. This is seen by the way in which these false teachers are destroying the faith of some people (v 18).
- **v 26:** Paul describes this false teaching as "the trap of the devil". God's enemy uses such false teaching to take people "captive to do his will".

Why does he take these distortions so seriously? From these descriptions, it is clear that Paul takes false teaching very seriously because, far from being just another point of view, this teaching is actually doing the work of the devil and endangering the eternal destiny of those who are taken in by it. Confronting this teaching is therefore a matter of life and death.

4. Pick out the three things this false teaching will do in v 16, 17 and 18.

- **v 16:** It causes people to become more and more ungodly ie: it affects how people act as well as how they think.
- **v 17:** It will spread—there are always people who find false teaching attractive.
- **v 18:** The faith of some will be destroyed.

5. APPLY: If people start to believe that there is no future bodily resurrection, because resurrection of some sort has already taken place... The aim of this question is to help people see that false teaching, which some may consider to be "just ideas", actually does have an effect on Christian behaviour, on other people and on the faith of people who are influenced by it.

- **why will that lead to ungodly behaviour?** If the resurrection has already taken place, there is no better future to look forward to—Christians have everything that they are going to get now. But if that is true, there is no longer any incentive to endure the hardship of self-denial, ridicule, opposition and persecution that Christians are called to suffer. If we get everything in this life, people will want to make sure that they get it all now—they will follow their feelings and do what they want, rather than what God wants.

- **why will others find that an attractive teaching?** It will be attractive to those who feel intimidated by modern "scientific" opinion about the resurrection, or who dislike the way in which belief in a bodily resurrection means that they may be ridiculed by non-believers.

- **why will that destroy the faith of some people?** If there is no bodily resurrection from death, what is the point of being a Christian? God does not have sovereign power because He cannot overcome death, or He does not love His people because He refuses to rescue them from death. Either way, there is not much point in listening to Him.

6. APPLY: What other kinds of false teaching might we be in danger from today? Having understood how serious the consequences of false teaching are, it is also important that your group is aware of current examples of false teaching. If people don't have any ideas, you may need to get the ball rolling eg: people are basically good, not sinners; Jesus didn't die on the cross; Jesus wasn't punished by God when He died on the cross; Jesus is just one of many ways to God; God doesn't know what is going to happen in the future (open theism); etc.

EXPLORE MORE

Read Matthew 7 v 15-23. What does the picture of wolves in sheep's clothing (v 15) tell us about these people? False teachers are very dangerous, but they look harmless—they wear sheep's clothing. We mustn't expect to identify them easily. They will look the part of a godly Christian leader.

How can we recognise false teachers? We can only recognise them by the bad fruit they produce (v 16).

How long will it take us to recognise them? What are the implications of this? It takes time for fruit to develop, so we probably won't be able to identify a false teacher immediately. The implications of this are that churches should spend time getting to know new people, and take the time to see the fruit of their lives, before they are entrusted with leading and teaching.

What kind of things can mislead us into thinking that someone is a godly

Christian? People are often misled by those who prophesy, or perform miracles or exorcisms, but some who do these things in the name of Jesus will be judged by Him as evildoers, so they are not a reliable indicator of true Christian faith.

What is the one thing that shows us whether someone is a true follower of Christ? Only if someone does the will of the Father (v 21) can we be sure that they are a true follower of Christ, ie: they listen to Jesus and do what He says. Eg: from the Beatitudes (5 v 3-12) a false teacher might look like the following: someone who is proud, complacent about sin, jealous for their rights, uninterested in righteousness, lacking in mercy, impure, fond of stirring up arguments and someone who avoids persecution.

7. By contrast with these false teachers, what should be Timothy's aim as a Christian teacher (v 15)? To handle correctly God's word so that he will be approved by God. This means helping God's people to understand God's message (the Bible) in the way that God intended it. Notice that if Timothy does this, he will not need to be ashamed; in other words, if he doesn't correctly handle God's word, then he should be ashamed. There are good reasons why Christians should sometimes be ashamed, but, as with Timothy, we often feel ashamed of ourselves or others for the wrong reasons—because of opposition and suffering for the gospel.

8. Look at v 14-16 and 23-26. Pick out the specific instructions that Paul gives to Timothy on how to handle false teaching. Timothy needs to remind people of "these things" (v 14). Make sure people look back to the preceding verses to find out what "these things" are—the truth about

Jesus Christ and the promises and warnings of the gospel (v 8-13). He must also warn people who are involved in pointless and damaging quarrels (v 14). He must correctly handle God's word (v 15), he must be able to teach (v 24) and "gently instruct" even those who oppose him (v 25). He should avoid godless chatter, which leads people into ungodliness (v 16, v 23-24).

When you have identified all the instructions in this passage, you may like to think about what all this will involve for a Christian leader. Eg: leaders need to be aware of who they are talking to and what they are saying. There will be some conversations that they have to get out of (godless chatter). There are people they will have to talk to, even when they really don't feel like it (instructing those who oppose them). Sometimes they will have to interfere in others' conversations (warning against quarrels). They will often have to keep saying the same things over and over (reminding people). There will be times when they should keep their opinions to themselves (avoid quarrelling). This will give your group a better idea of some of the pressures involved in Christian leadership.

- **What should Timothy's aim be in his dealings with those spreading false teaching?** To see these "problem people" repent and grow in knowledge of the truth, so that they can escape the trap of the devil (v 25). Notice how this shows the urgency and importance of Paul's instructions—eternal destinies are at stake here. Also notice how this will affect Timothy's attitude towards those who oppose him—if Timothy remembers this aim as he instructs and warns them, he is much more likely to be mature, gentle and pure in the way he acts towards them.

9. APPLY: How can we help our gospel

teachers to deal with false teaching and people who are influenced by it?
Get your group to think of practical ways in which they can help their church leaders to do some of the things outlined in question 8 above. Here are some questions that your group may find useful:

• How much importance do I place on leaders teaching God's word? Do I accept they need adequate time for Bible study and preparation, or do I pressure them to get involved in other things?

• How do I respond when church leaders spend time explaining basic gospel truths that I already know? Do I get bored, or complain that no one is meeting my needs? Or do I support them in what they are doing, recognising my own need to be reminded of the gospel, and doing what I can to reinforce gospel teaching in my own conversations with other Christians?

• What's my reaction when church leaders confront people in the church over false teaching? Am I likely to criticise them without knowing all the facts? Is my response influenced by gossip and rumour? Or do I seek to trust them and, if necessary, go to them for an explanation.
See also v 19 for Paul's encouragement to Timothy. He reminds Timothy that despite the false teachers, "God's solid foundation [of His worldwide church] stands firm" (v 19). Timothy can be reassured because, despite the confusion false teaching causes, God knows who truly belongs to Him (and who does not). But there is also a challenge for those who say they follow God—they must turn away from any type of wickedness, including false teaching. Get your group to think about how they might use v 19 to encourage their church leaders.

10. Why might Timothy (and we) need to hear Paul's warning...

• **to cleanse himself from ignoble purposes (v 21)?** He himself might be tempted to give in and follow the false teaching—either because he finds it attractive, or just because it would make life easier for him.

• **to flee the evil desires of youth (v 22)?** He might also try to fight the false teaching in an immature way.

⊻

• **What does a mature response to false teaching look like (v 22-25)?** It comes from someone who joins with other true Christians in pursuing righteousness, faith, love and peace (v 22); it involves refusing to join in with quarrels (v 23); being kind and not resentful (v 24); being gentle with opponents (v 25).

11. From v 23-26, try to sum up what Timothy's overall strategy should be towards both false teachers and to those prepared to argue over much less serious issues. He should avoid arguments about things which are not important (v 23). However, he must oppose serious false teaching (v 25)—but he must do this in a gentle way (v 25-26). In fact, he must deal kindly with the whole congregation.

• **Why was it important for Timothy both to stand up against false views and yet to do this gently?** Because they would destroy people's faith—not to do so would be unloving to those whose eternal destinies were threatened by such teaching. But it needs to be gentle, to win people back, not just win the argument.

12. APPLY: If we come across false teaching in our church, what should we do? And what should we avoid doing? This last question gives the group an opportunity to review everything that has been said in the session. As a fun alternative, you may like to tackle the case-study given in the optional extra below.

Note: As we have seen, false teaching is a deadly serious issue, and if it is clearly being spread around a congregation, the matter needs to be dealt with by the church leadership as a whole, with the support of all the church ie: it will probably not be appropriate for one Christian to tackle on their own. On the other hand, a mature Christian may come across a newer or less mature Christian who has recently heard dodgy teaching and is confused or doesn't recognise the threat. In this situation, informal one-to-one biblical instruction and encouragement from the more mature Christian may be appropriate.

OPTIONAL EXTRA

Adapt the following case-study to your own type of church…

JUST IMAGINE… St Athanasius, East Tootwich / Tootwich Community Church looks like a fairly typical church, where a friend of yours, Joe Bloggs, has just got the job of vicar/minister. It doesn't take him long to find out that there are a few "issues":

• On Monday morning he receives several letters from people worried by a sermon given by a lay-reader/elder on Sunday, titled "Why the virgin birth didn't happen" (a follow-up to his Easter sermon, which gave the resurrection similar treatment).

• On Tuesday evening, a home-group leader tries to draw him into the "153 debate", which has been raging for a month (about the significance of the number of fish caught by the disciples in John 20).

• While visiting the Wednesday Fellowship (mainly for older people), he walks into the middle of the "cups or mugs?" argument, caused by the £100 left in Mrs Smith's will,

with the instruction that it was to be used to "purchase suitable crockery".

• During Thursday (his day off!) he gets phone calls from members of the choir (who wear robes!) and the worship band (who play drums!), asking which will be leading the first hymn/song on Sunday.

• Now he has just returned from the Friday evening youth group, who want to go to "Explode", a huge (and very trendy) event run by an American evangelist, who does preach the gospel, though he throws in his own bizarre ideas as well.

Joe e-mails you for advice. He is preaching his first sermon on Sunday, and the church will be packed with people excited to know what he will say. On Monday he has organised meetings with the leaders of various groups, followed by his first PCC/elders' meeting, a chance to set out his vision for the church. He wants to know where he should start, and he needs you to e-mail back right now! Fortunately you have been doing a really helpful series of Bible studies on 2 Timothy, which seem strangely relevant. You have just a couple of minutes to glance through your notes before you type a reply. What would you say?

Some suggestions: Positively, he must start by making sure he preaches the truth (v 15). Negatively, he has to speak to the lay-reader/elder—this is a serious issue (v 25-26). He probably also needs to check out "Explode" and find out what exactly are the American preacher's "bizarre ideas", in order to assess whether there is an issue of false teaching there. He shouldn't get involved in the "silly" arguments—the "153" debate, the "cups or mugs" argument and the tensions between the choir and worship band. In fact, he may have to tell others to stop arguing (v 14). Some issues may be worth dealing with at some stage, but not at the moment when there are more serious things to sort out.

6 2 Timothy 3
CHOOSING A GODLY LIFE

THE BIG IDEA

Difficult times, because of the wrong attitudes of some in the church, are to be expected. We need to hold to the gospel message and the lifestyle of true gospel ministers like Paul.

SUMMARY

Paul first explains that godless attitudes are to be expected—even within the church (v 1-6). This will lead some people to carry out godless ministry (v 6-9). However, the attitudes and ministry Timothy has seen from Paul stand in stark contrast to these "evil men" (v 10-13). Timothy must choose between these two role models. He should hold on to the message he has heard from Paul, and base his own ministry on it, because he knows the character of those (like Paul) who told him this message. And he knows this message is from the Scriptures—which is the only basis of godly ministry (v 14-17).

In this session, people will be challenged to be discerning about those who appear to be godly, by seeing how the behaviour of these people matches up with their words, how their Christian language matches up with the teaching of the Bible, and whether, in their ministry, they stick with the gospel and endure suffering. People will be presented with reasons why they should choose a godly life, even though this involves hardship and persecution—because of the godly lives of those from whom they have received the gospel, and because of the God-breathed Scriptures, which brought them to Christ. The application questions encourage people to give a high priority both to belonging

to a good church and to effective Bible ministry—informally as they influence others around them, and formally in the meetings, programmes and ministries of their church.

OPTIONAL EXTRA

Good Christian biographies can be a great source of inspiration, just as Paul's life, ministry and sufferings were to Timothy. Bring a selection to share (make sure there is some variety—short and longer biographies, historical and modern ones, testimonies from abroad as well as home, ordinary Christians as well as leaders, women as well as men.) Or, if appropriate, ask people to share about someone whose Christian life has inspired and strengthened them in the gospel.

GUIDANCE ON QUESTIONS

1. How easily are you taken in by appearances? Talk about an occasion when your first impressions of someone, based on their appearance, turned out to be quite wrong. This question is designed to prepare for the first part of this session, which deals with the reality of people in our churches who have an appearance of godliness but whose hearts are full of the evils listed in verses 2-5. We know that we can be misled by false impressions in other areas of life, and yet we can still be gullible when it comes to discerning the true state of those who say they are Christians—young people, new believers and immature Christians may be particularly at risk. It is important that we all hear Paul's warning to Timothy about the kind of people who can sometimes worm their way into a Christian group.

- **How do we come to see the truth behind someone's misleading appearance?** When we realise that their behaviour does not match up to their words. This takes time; it also means that we should not only listen to what people say, but watch what they do, and not only in public but also in private, when they think that no one is watching them.

2. The phrase "lovers of…" begins and finishes the list. Compare the two phrases. What is at the heart of the wrong attitudes described here? Human selfishness—people putting themselves and their own desires before what God wants for them. (The same phrase is used in for "not lovers of good"—v 3).

⊻

- **Take a moment to read through the rest of the list. Which would be most disturbing for you to find in your church?** Some in your group, especially new Christians or young people, may be shocked at the idea of finding people in the church who fit these descriptions. New Christians are often thrilled at finding a local family of Christian believers, who may compare very favourably with their non-Christian family, friends or work colleagues. Thankfully, they have so far not experienced ungodliness in the lives of those who say that they are Christians but don't live a Christian life. However, it is important for them to be prepared by Paul's words here, because sooner or later, they will come across people like this.

3. These people have a form of godliness (they look godly), but deny its power (v 5). What is the power that they deny (compare 1 v 8)? In 1 v 8, the

power of God will enable Timothy to join with Paul in teaching about Jesus Christ and suffering for the gospel, without being shamed into giving up this work.

- **What might these people look like in our churches today?** These are people who seem to be godly—they do what Christians do (eg: go to church services) and they use what appears to be Christian language. But actually they are not involved in true Christian ministry, which is about teaching the gospel and being prepared to suffer for it. They use Christian language, but actually they mean something different from what the Bible means (eg: "resurrection" as used by Hymenaeus and Philetus in 2 v 18.) They do not have God's power to endure as true Christians ie: to endure in believing and teaching the gospel through opposition and hardship.

4. How do these people operate in their "ministry" (v 6-7)? They pick on the most vulnerable people—those who feel a real need for God's forgiveness, or are susceptible to temptation—but their "ministry" never leads these people to God's truth. It's manipulative but it's not effective! **Note:** Paul is not saying in v 6 that all women are weak-willed, but that these ungodly people will make a bee-line for those who are weak-willed. It may be that women were particularly vulnerable in Paul's day because their lives were generally regulated by the men in their families and communities—ie: they were unaccustomed to making their own decisions—and they were least likely to have had any education.

5. What comfort can Timothy take from the way Paul finishes this section of his letter in v 8-9? God knows about these people (even if they fool others), and He has rejected them! And in the end, the fact that their ministry is not from God will become clear, even if they deceive people for a time. **Note:** It is not certain precisely who Jannes and Jambres were (v 8). Some think they were the Egyptian magicians who opposed Moses (eg: Exodus 7 v 11). Others think that they are the traditional names of those who led the rebellion against Moses recorded in Numbers 16. The key point is that even in the time of Moses, there were people who opposed godly and God-appointed leaders.

EXPLORE MORE

Read Acts 4 v 23-31. What have these Christians understood about opposition to God's work? They have understood that those who had opposed God, like Herod and Pontius Pilate, could only do what His power and will had decided beforehand should happen (v 28). **Having experienced persecution, what do they pray for?** Confident that everything is under God's control, they don't pray for persecution to stop but instead ask God to help them keep teaching the gospel with great boldness (v 29). **What is the result?** They are filled with the Holy Spirit, and they speak the word of God boldly (v 31).

EXPLORE MORE

What happened?
Acts 5 v 11-14: Although everybody was seized with great fear (v 11), and non-believers didn't dare join the Christians in their meetings (v 13), more and more people became Christians (v 14).
Acts 5 v 41 – 6 v 1: The apostles were filled with joy and continued to teach the gospel, and the number of disciples increased (6 v 1).
Acts 6 v 7: The word of God spread and the church grew rapidly.

What happened?
Acts 8 v 1-4: All of the church, except the apostles, were scattered throughout Judea and Samaria, but they preached the word of God wherever they went (8 v 4). (See 8 v 14 to find out what happened in Samaria.)

6. Timothy has worked with Paul and seen the way in which he goes about his gospel ministry. Contrast Paul with the people who have just been described (v 10-11). Paul gives a list of the characteristics of his ministry. Notice that the first four things mentioned—his teaching, his way of life, his purpose and his faith—are the basis for everything Paul does. The next three things—his patience, love and endurance—describe his attitude to people and situations. Get people to contrast these with the characteristics of the ungodly ministers mentioned in v 1-5; eg: Paul loves others, but the false teachers love themselves (v 2). Finally, Paul makes another strong contrast between himself and these people, by mentioning the persecutions (from people) and hardships (from the lifestyle that goes with his ministry) that he has suffered. Compare the false ministers ("lovers of pleasure"—v 4)—they certainly don't let themselves suffer!

7. What sobering fact must Timothy face up to as he makes the choice to live a godly life (v 11-13)? Paul's way of life, which includes hardship, is actually normal for Christians who want to please God. This doesn't mean that all Christians will suffer as much as he did all of the time, but that sometimes we will face hardships, and we should always be prepared for this.

8. Timothy should continue with what he knows to be true (v 14, 15). What

are the two reasons why he can stick confidently with this teaching?

- **v 14:** Timothy knows well the people he has heard this message from—he has seen the lives of Paul and others, and knows they live out the message. When you compare the lives of the false ministers, why would you abandon the Paul's message for one preached by proud, unloving, treacherous manipulators?
- **v 15:** Timothy knows the Scriptures through and through. (For him, this was the Old Testament, which his mother and grandmother had taught him—for us, it's the whole Bible.) So he can see that Paul's message is consistent with, and based on Scripture. And Scripture itself is enough to bring people to trust in Jesus for salvation, as Timothy has experienced himself. If the message of Scripture can bring about this destiny-transforming miracle of faith in Christ, why would you turn to the message of the false ministers instead?

9. APPLY: Many people today believe that you can be a Christian without needing to belong to a church. Having read Paul's words here, how would you answer this from verses 10-15? A good church is where we can find the two encouragements to continue in the faith that Paul has reminded Timothy of—the lives of those who live out the gospel, and the Scriptures, which make us "wise for salvation through faith in Christ Jesus". As we have seen in Paul's letter to Timothy so far, the pressures on Christians can be immense—Paul thought that Timothy, even though he had been brought up in a godly home, needed the Scriptures and the godly examples of true gospel-focused Christians to encourage him to continue in the Christian faith. We live in a society where the gospel is ridiculed, undermined and opposed by those both inside and outside church. To those who say that they are Christians but don't need church, we should ask: What makes you think that you are stronger than Timothy?

10. Think about the four things that Scripture is useful for (v 16). Link these four uses of Scripture with instructions that Paul has already given Timothy.

- **Teaching:** 1 v 13—"What you heard from me, keep as the pattern of sound teaching"; 2 v 15—one who "correctly handles the word of truth".
- **Rebuking:** 2 v 14—"Warn them before God against quarrelling about words".
- **Correcting:** 2 v 25—"Those who oppose him he must gently instruct, in the hope that God will grant them repentance leading them to a knowledge of the truth".
- **Training in righteousness:** 2 v 2—"The things you have heard me say in the presence of many witnesses entrust to reliable men who will also be qualified to teach others".

- **How does using Scripture in these ways give Timothy a balanced ministry?** Teaching and training are positive aspects of Bible ministry, helping people to go further along the right path. Rebuking and correcting are negative aspects of Bible ministry—they seek to stop people going down the wrong path and to turn them onto the right one. People need to know where they are going wrong (rebuking). But that alone is no good, unless they know how to change (correcting). But then they are likely to go wrong again if they don't know the right way (teaching). Finally, they need to become mature so that they too can be used by God to help others in sticking to the gospel (training in righteousness). Without all four of these aspects, Bible ministry will be weak and ineffective.

11. Surely Timothy knows Scripture is God-breathed. So why does he now need reminding of this, do you think? If Scripture is going to be the basis of Timothy's ministry, and his weapon against false teaching, he needs to remember that it is true and powerful—it's GOD speaking, not just him!

12. APPLY: Are there any ways in which we should change the way we use Scripture in the light of these verses, both individually and as a church? In discussing this application, you could give the group these questions to think about:
• Do we remember that the Bible is God's word? Is that reflected in the priority that God's word is given in church meetings, ministries and programmes? And in our own daily schedules, our conversations, our thinking about the things that happen around us, our decision-making, etc.
• Do we base our ministry to others around the Bible, so that they hear God and not just us? (This might mean referring to the Bible more often in our conversations with people in church. And it might mean re-assessing how much the Bible is used in ministries such as youth work or Sunday school, marriage prep, counselling, etc.)
• Do we have the right balance between teaching, training, rebuking and correcting? Is there any part of our church teaching programme that deals with false teaching? Do church leaders ever challenge the congregation to repent of specific wrongs that have been identified in Bible teaching? Does the church do anything to help Christians who want to grow in their faith?
• Are we confident that Bible ministry can thoroughly equip Christians for every good work, or are we tempted to turn to other ideas and programmes for help?

7 2 Timothy 4
FINISHING THE RACE

THE BIG IDEA
We have to make the choice between telling people what they want to hear or preaching the true gospel message, as Paul has done (which will bring opposition, desertion and suffering). But only if we follow Paul's example will we finish the race and receive the crown of righteousness.

SUMMARY
Chapter 4 concludes Paul's letter. He revisits many of the major themes he has been speaking about, and reminds Timothy of what is most important. This session should be used as an opportunity to review what has been learned throughout the course. Don't worry if you end up feeling that everything has been said before—it's likely that we are meant to feel that.

In the final chapter of his letter, Paul gives a list of commands (v 2 and 5) that are like a bullet-point summary of everything he has instructed Timothy to do. But he places these commands in the context of the long-term view (v 1)—the constant all-seeing presence of Christ and His unstoppable appearing on the last day, when He will judge everyone and bring in His kingdom. That's what makes following these commands so worthwhile. And he reminds Timothy of the immediate situation that he faces (v 3-4)—the continued presence and even "success" of the false teachers. That's what makes responding to these commands so urgent.

Finally, before finishing off with personal comments, requests and items of news (v 9-22), Paul gives his verdict on his own life and ministry of labour and suffering for the gospel (v 6-8). He uses three images of his life—a drink offering, a good fight and a race—each of which have helped him to endure hardship and remain faithful to the Lord. Now approaching the end of his life, Paul can show Timothy that even in such a stressful and difficult life and ministry as Paul's, the Lord stays faithful to His promise that He will bring His children safely to His heavenly kingdom. If that is true of Paul, then surely it can be true of Timothy as well.

This session challenges people to view life as Paul did—as an offering to God, a good fight that must be fought, and a race that needs to be run. This will help us to endure hardship, remain faithful to the Lord and do gospel work both in and out of season. People are encouraged to reflect on where they face the fiercest struggle between "keeping the faith" and "suiting their own desires", and to review what they have learned from this Bible-study course which will help them to stay faithful to the end.

GUIDANCE ON QUESTIONS

1. Forrest Gump said: "Life is like a box of chocolates—you never know what you're going to get!" Think of some popular images of life. How do you think these images may affect the way people live their lives? The purpose of this question is to show the importance and power of the images that people have of their lives. Paul himself uses three images in verses 6-7 to sum up the gospel-centred way in which he has lived his life; Q8 will look at how Paul's view of his life has helped him to endure and suffer. The challenge of this session will be to make us ask ourselves what we, as Christians, expect our lives to be about. Some common ideas about life (and the implications) include:

- Life is a journey: this usually emphasises the idea that you should make progress as you go through life—strangely people are often not very confident of or interested in where you will end up at the end!
- Life is a struggle for survival: this notion may be born out of personal experience, or, more philosophically, come from evolution—it assumes that each person must be tough and should look out for themselves. Helping others may be seen as weak and stupid according to some who hold this view of life.
- Life is a human right: while no one is likely to disagree with this statement, a rights-based view of life can lead to a culture in which everyone expects to get, but no one wants to work for, wait for or give anything back.
- Life is a circle: this idea comes from eastern religion—a pessimistic view of life as a circle would emphasise that there can never be any progress; an optimistic view would believe that there is always another chance to get things right.

As an alternative way of tackling this question, read out the following quotes about life, and ask people how these views might affect the people who believe them.

- "Life is a foreign language."

- "Life is just one thing after another."
- "Life's a b***h and then you die."
- "Life is a fatal complaint—and an eminently contagious one."
- "Life is a sexually-transmitted disease."
- "Life is what happens to you while you're busy making other plans" (John Lennon).

2. What is the long-term view that Timothy must keep in mind as he listens to Paul's final instructions (v 1)? He must remember four main things: God's presence with His people; the fact that Jesus is the judge; the fact that Jesus will appear again (ie: return); the fact that Jesus will rule God's kingdom. Note that all these four things are mentioned again during chapter 4—God's presence in v 17, Jesus as judge and His appearing in v 8, and Jesus' kingdom in v 18. From this we can see that the long-term view was not just some "blessed thought" that Paul had decided would be nice to put into his letter, but truth which he always had in view, and which had influenced his decisions, choices, actions and endurance.

- **In what way is this both the greatest encouragement and the biggest warning that Timothy could have?** Timothy should be warned against not taking his gospel ministry seriously by the fact that everything he does is seen by Jesus, who will return to judge him and everyone else. But he can also be comforted by knowing Jesus is always with Him and can bring him into His kingdom.

3. In contrast to the long-term view, the immediate situation facing Timothy is false teaching. In verses 3-4, what characteristic marks out false teaching and those who follow it? False teaching tells people what they want to hear, and those who follow it do so because they like

what they hear. The implications of this are that false teachers will seem to have success because of their popularity (although 3 v 9 assures us that this will be temporary).

4. APPLY: How can these verses help us to choose which church leaders we should listen to? We should be careful not to listen to people because they say what we want to hear, but to listen to those who teach from God's word—this will often make us feel uncomfortable!

5. List all of Paul's commands in verses 2 and 5. How will understanding both the long-term view (Q2) and the immediate outlook (Q3) help Timothy to carry out each of these instructions? Get your group to pick out the nine imperatives ("do" words) in these verses, and as you list them, talk about how understanding the long-term view and the immediate situation can help Timothy to carry out these instructions.

- "Preach the Word" (v 2)—only God's word can save people from the judgment of God at the end of history.
- "Be prepared" (v 2)—false teaching will make the task of preaching God's word difficult and discouraging, so don't be surprised when it happens.
- "Correct, rebuke and encourage" (v 2)—as we saw in 3 v 16-17, only by using God's word to correct, rebuke and encourage can people be turned from false teaching, and helped to stick to the true gospel.
- "Keep your head" (v 5)—the false teachers will seem to have success because their message is popular, but don't panic, because the ultimate judge of success in gospel ministry will be Jesus Christ.
- "Endure hardship" (v 5)—Jesus Christ is always with you and will one day give you a crown of righteousness.
- "Do the work of an evangelist" (v 5)—

Jesus Christ will come again to judge everyone, so nothing is more important than helping people to come to salvation before that day.

- "Discharge all the duties of your ministry" (v 5)—it may seem that no one notices what you do, but God sees everything, so don't become slack in your gospel ministry.

6. How do these verses sum up what Paul has been encouraging Timothy to do throughout the letter? Timothy is to do the job of a church leader, which God gave him the gifts to do (1 v 6). He is to guard the true gospel message that he heard from Paul (1 v 13-14), and to make sure this is passed on (2 v 2). This is the message based on Scripture (3 v 14-16)—"preach the Word" and "do the work of an evangelist". Timothy is to do this knowing that this gospel has brought Paul persecution from those outside the church (eg: 2 v 8-9 and 3 v 11-12), and that it is also under attack from many inside the church (2 v 17-18 and 3 v 1-9). So Timothy too must expect hardship as he does his job (1 v 8 and 2 v 3)—"endure hardship" and "be prepared in season and out of season". But he must remain kind and gentle as he tries to correct those who have gone wrong (2 v 24-25)—"correct, rebuke and encourage". So overall, he must not be ashamed of the gospel or of Paul (1 v 8), and trust that, in the end, the power of God's word will do its work of bringing people to know God (2 v 9 and 3 v 15)—"keep your head" and "discharge all the duties of your ministry".

7. APPLY: What does it mean for us to be prepared to do these things "in season and out of season"? Doing them whenever we can. Doing them "out of season" will be both when others don't

want to listen, and when we don't feel like speaking. You could ask your group to share some recent "out of season" moments—get started with an example of your own.

8. In v 6 and 7, Paul uses three images of the Christian life. What are they? And how have they helped Paul to endure hardship and remain faithful to the Lord?

- **v 6:** A drink offering being poured out—a drink offering was a gift of wine made to God and poured out alongside an Old Testament animal sacrifice (see Numbers 15 v 1-12). "Throwing away" the best wine might appear to some people to be a sorry waste, but every Jew would have understood the worth of an offering to God. Similarly, many might conclude that imprisonment was a waste of Paul's life and talents, but Paul knows that because his life is an offering to God, it can never be wasted.

- **v 7a:** A good fight—a fight involves struggle, and it is a matter of life and death. A person who views their life as a good fight is prepared for, not surprised by, struggle, and is willing to throw all their effort, ability and resources into that struggle. From the time that he became a Christian and was called to go and preach the gospel to the Gentiles, Paul knew that his life would be a tough and painful one, but there could be no other way.

- **v 7b:** A race—in a race you go through sweat and pain to reach your goal—the winning post. In living life as if running a race, Paul always kept his eyes on the finishing post (see 4 v 1, 8 and 18). The hope of his reward kept him going.

9. How does Paul's situation make his commands even more important? Paul realises that his death ("departure"—v 6) will come relatively soon (though v 9-12 suggest he is hoping for one final meeting with his most trusted fellow-workers first). It is now time for Timothy and others to pass the gospel message on to the next generation.

10. How will Paul's testimony here be an encouragement to Timothy? Paul has managed to stay faithful to Jesus and His gospel right to the end (v 7), and so he trusts Jesus' promise of being right with God ("crown of righteousness") on the final judgment day (v 8). In Paul's life and ministry, Timothy can see that Jesus is faithful to His promises.

11. From [v 9-22], pick out examples of…
- **the way most people inside the church treated Paul:** Demas seems to have deserted Paul because he has stopped believing (v 10—"loved this world"; compare 3 v 2-4); others have deserted him in his hour of need, maybe because it seemed too costly to them, though they are still believers (v 16).

- **opposition from those outside the church:** Alexander opposed the gospel message (v 14). Paul is willing to leave it up to God to judge him on this matter; it's not his job to get revenge.

- **Paul's suffering for the gospel message:** Paul's loneliness, his hardship in prison (v 13), and his time in court (v 16).

- **Paul's confidence in the Lord for the future:** v 18—as in v 8, Paul talks about his ultimate salvation. Whatever people do to him, Christ will keep him safe eternally.

12. APPLY: In what area of your life (as a church and as individual Christians) do you see the fiercest struggle taking place between "keeping the faith" (v 7) and "suiting your own desires" (v 3)? This question is an opportunity for people to share personally how they might be standing in Timothy's shoes. Hopefully, the group will have grown together throughout these Bible studies, and will feel able to share their difficulties, and seek prayer and encouragement from one another.

13. APPLY: Now that we have reached the end of 2 Timothy, what has been the biggest encouragement (or warning) for you to stay faithful to the true gospel? Make sure that people don't just share difficulties but also lessons learned, encouragements and answers to prayer.

EXPLORE MORE
Read Revelation 22 v 12-21. John's last written words share similar concerns with those of Paul—Jesus Christ (who He is and what He will do when He returns), the Christian hope, and the problem of false teachers.
What does John say about these things?
Jesus Christ: John quotes the words of Jesus Himself. Jesus is coming back (soon!)
- He will bring a reward and He will judge everyone according to what they have done (v 12)—compare 2 Timothy 4 v 1 and 8.
- Jesus calls Himself the "Alpha and Omega", 'First and Last", "Beginning and End" (v 13) ie: He is God. Compare 2 Timothy 1 v 9—Jesus was there before time began, when God's gift of grace was first planned.
- In Revelation 22, Jesus also calls Himself the Root and Offspring of David (v 16) ie: both the one from whom David originated (His creator), and the descendant of David—compare 2 Timothy 2 v 8.

- He also calls Himself the bright Morning Star (v 16). ie: a star that heralds the dawn of a new day. Compare 2 Timothy 1 v 11—Jesus has destroyed death and brought life and immortality to light through the gospel; see also 2 v 8—Jesus has already been raised from the dead. When He returns and brings His reward, we too shall be raised from the dead to enjoy life and immortality for ever.

The Christian hope: Those who wash their robes have the right to the tree of life and to go into the city (God's kingdom) (v 14). Compare 2 Timothy 1 v 9-10—in Jesus Christ we have been saved and called to a holy life (see also 2 v 19); compare 4 v 18—those in Christ who are faithful to the end, as Paul was, will be brought safely to Christ's heavenly kingdom.

False teachers: God will judge them and they will not enter His kingdom (v 18-19). Compare Paul's verdict on them—they destroy people's faith (2 v 18), they are caught in a trap of the devil (2 v 26), they are rejected and they will not get very far (3 v 8-9); along with everyone, they will be judged by Jesus Christ (4 v 1).

How can we be encouraged by the "same mind" that Paul and John shared? The fact that Paul and John, writing in different times and places, share a "common mind" can encourage us greatly to be confident in the truth of the gospel, and in the reliability of the Scriptures, which speak, not as 66 separate documents, but as one book, authored by God.

OPTIONAL EXTRA

At the end of the session, or as a follow-up session, give your group 30-40 minutes to work out a presentation of 2 Timothy for an imaginary audience of people who know nothing about Paul's letter. This could be done in the form of a drama, a news report, a song, rap or poem, a quiz etc. Allow people to be creative in choosing the style of their presentation, but the content should be based on the main points of the seven sessions of this course that you have studied together. As well as being a fun activity, it can help people to realise both how much they have learned and also the value of passing that on to others.

Some other titles in the Good Book Guide series...

OLD TESTAMENT

Genesis 1 – 4: In the beginning
7 studies. ISBN: 9781907377112

Ruth: Poverty and plenty
4 studies. ISBN: 9781905564910

1 Kings: the rise and fall of King Solomon 8 studies.
ISBN: 9781907377976

Jonah: The depths of grace
6 studies. ISBN: 9781907377433

NEW TESTAMENT

Mark 1 – 8: The coming King
10 studies. ISBN: 9781904889281

1 Peter: Living in the real world
5 studies. ISBN: 9781907377853

1 John: How to be sure
7 studies. ISBN: 9781904889953

Revelation 2 – 3: A message from Jesus to the church today
7 studies. ISBN: 9781905564682

Visit your local website to see the full Good Book Guide range, and to download samples
UK & Europe: www.thegoodbook.co.uk • North America: www.thegoodbook.com
Australia: www.thegoodbook.com.au • New Zealand: www.thegoodbook.co.nz